128" MAR

W9-BVT-132

PROBLEMATIC MAN

PROBLEMATIC MAN

Gabriel Marcel

TRANSLATED BY
BRIAN THOMPSON

HERDER AND HERDER

1967
HERDER AND HERDER NEW YORK
232 Madison Avenue, New York 10016

Original edition: *L'Homme problématique,*
Paris, Aubier.

Contents

FOREWORD, BY LESLIE DEWART   7

PART ONE   PROBLEMATIC MAN   15

PART TWO   HUMAN UNEASINESS   65

     I. UNEASINESS, ANXIETY, ANGUISH   67

     II. THE UNEASY PERSON AS SELF-TORMENTOR   72

     III. UNEASINESS CONDEMNED BY THE SAGES   78

     IV. UNEASINESS IN THE PERSPECTIVE OF THE GOSPEL   84

     V. UNEASINESS IN ST. AUGUSTINE   90

     VI. UNEASINESS IN PASCAL   96

     VII. FROM PASCAL TO KIERKEGAARD   101

     VIII. FROM KIERKEGAARD TO NIETZSCHE AND HEIDEGGER   107

     IX. FROM HEIDEGGER TO SARTRE   113

     X. GOETHE AND UNEASINESS OVERCOME   119

     XI. UNEASINESS IN ANDRÉ GIDE   125

     XII. UNEASINESS IN THE WORLD OF TODAY   131

CONCLUSION   138

5

Foreword

By Leslie Dewart

THE integration of human experience and Christian belief is hardly a novel problem for the Christian world. It is, in fact, a perennial task. There is no reason to believe that some day it will have been accomplished once for all. For not only human experience evolves constantly; the Christian faith too must undergo continuous development both in the individual and in the corporation of believers as a whole. Since belief itself is a type of experience, a reality of the same order as every other experience, it too naturally tends to develop historically following the same processes which are at work in the cultural evolution of man.

Hence, the most common expression used to refer to this problem, "the integration of experience and faith," is doubly misleading. The task is not to render two things into one. For, in the first place, faith and experience are not dichotomous; and, in the second, they should not be made into an undifferentiated whole. As Brian Wicker has pointed out in *Toward a Contemporary Christianity* (Notre Dame, 1967), faith *is* the fundamental meaningfulness of experience. To integrate faith and experience is nothing else than to interpret experience *truthfully*, that is, to

7

derive truth from experience: "the fundamental problem to be solved, whether it be couched in terms of a return to Christianity or in terms of a new kind of secularism, is that of making sense of our experience in the new setting [of contemporary human existence, a setting definable by] the unique historical possibility of a totally humanised and controlled world." Thus, to make sense out of everyday experience is the Christian vocation "which the very humanisation we have brought about demands of us. If the world is to be one of increasingly human control, the problem is that of finding an intellectual basis upon which to understand the meanings which this world offers us. This is the first priority—not the imposition of Christianity . . . but the discovery of a new kind of intelligibility."

Of course, these formulae could all too easily be given a "naturalistic" and "secularistic" sense, in the traditional Catholic acceptation of these terms. Yet, this view need not imply that faith, that is, religious experience, is reducible to non-religious, secular or "natural" experience. Quite the contrary, the point is that *ordinary* human experience is *insufficient* unto itself unless it extend itself into a new, extra-ordinary dimension. When it so extends itself it becomes religious experience or faith. The apparent opposition between faith *and* experience simply means: precisely insofar as experience is *immanent* in the being of man, experience has a *transcendent* dimension, namely, faith. In other words, faith transcends experience only because faith is the transcendence *of* experience. Faith is, as it were, the *ultimate* meaning of that which *already* exists. But this too may be misleading: in this context "ultimacy" should not carry the Hellenic connotation of *finality* but simply that of *futurity*. The idea is simply that experience as such already exists. But unless we understood experience "speculatively," as in the tradition that began with the pre-Socratics and extended to Hegel, we must understand it, to use Dewey's term, as "participation." But if experience is self-participation in being, man's self-constitution into being, it follows that the experience which already exists clamours, as it were, for a meaningfulness which it can only find *beyond itself*. Faith is precisely this transcendent, projective dimension of the presence of human consciousness to itself.

Now, signally among Catholic philosophers Gabriel Marcel has long devoted himself to the study of the integration of Christian faith and contemporary experience—I mean, the study of the transcendent meaning of human phenomena. For indeed this is what for him constitutes Christian philosophy. *Problematic Man* is especially valuable among Marcel's contributions, however, in that it deals with the problem at a much more basic level than he had previously done. This is true not only because in this work the foregoing understanding of the relations of faith and experience is most penetratingly perceived by him, but also because in this study Marcel realizes, with original insight, that this view of faith directly implies a proposition that Christian philosophers have long avoided: that there is something *fundamentally* valid (albeit also fundamentally distorted) in modern man's self-alienation from God—and consequently in modern man's experience of loneliness, anxiety and even nihilism. The quest for meaning, Marcel seems to say in this book, necessarily and properly implies a state of original meaninglessness. More generally: once experience questions itself, the experience of meaninglessness is the condition of the possibility of meaningfulness. It is no accident, no mere coincidence, that modern philosophical speculation—that is, in the last one hundred years or so—has produced "uneasiness." The question that arises for Christian philosophy once this historical fact has been accepted has to do with the nature, legitimacy and value of this stage of the history of philosophical experience. For instance, does "uneasiness" indicate that man's self-questioning logically and inevitably leads to nihilism?

Marcel considers very seriously the hypotheses which, almost as a conditioned reflex (as well they might be, after 150 years of uninterrupted Catholic conviction that contemporary man has already been judged by God and consigned to perdition), usually spring to the lips of the apologetic Catholic thinker. First, the primacy of faith over experience implies that any lack of integration between the two is to be overcome only by an adjustment *of experience to faith*—and not vice versa. Second, the lack of integration between theistic faith and contemporary experience is attributable to modern man having religiously disabled himself, that is, having rendered himself incapable of belief in God.

Marcel's findings are expressed in passages which may be counted among the most lucid and eloquent of his distinguished philosophical career. "It is not in our power," he says, "it is no longer even among our possibilities, to retrograde towards the stage in history in which man could appear to himself as an evident given." (Incidentally, this alone should make one wonder whether Marcel's supposed incompatibility with a Teilhardian perspective is not wholly illusory.) To the second he replies yet more forcefully: "It is perhaps not illegitimate to think that what is dead, what is out of date, is a certain manner of conceiving either God Himself, or, to speak more precisely, the specific mode of relation which unites me to this God to which I as man refer." And he explains: "I think we should have done with the idea of God as Cause, of a god concentrating in himself all causality, or even, in more rigorous terms, with all theological usage of the notion of causality. . . . It could be . . . that the God whose death Nietzsche truthfully announced was the god of the Aristotelian-Thomistic tradition, god the prime mover."

Thus free to evaluate positively the nature of the "uneasiness" produced by man's self-problematization, in the second part of this book Marcel proceeds to analyze this experience historically and phenomenologically. His conclusions are, once again, highly Teilhardian. They are, in any event, unquestionably relevant to the post-conciliar situation of the Church. Though "uneasiness" may well degenerate—and has in fact frequently degenerated—into the "anguish" of the existentialists, Marcel says, it need not do so. Though he would not wish to go "so far as to say that it is good in itself," he finds that "uneasiness" is legitimate and proper at a certain stage in the development of human consciousness: "the absence of uneasiness, except perhaps in the saint, is a serious symptom." Moreover, the Christian faith can render meaningful not only experience in general, but even this very uneasiness, this very meaninglessness which is the condition of the possibility of meaningfulness: "let us not conclude . . . that uneasiness can . . . be eliminated, but rather that it should be transmuted into an active disposition which partakes of faith. . . . But I would add that faith can by no means be conceived in a quietist sense, it must on the contrary stir as it were a continual invention."

11

In sum, despite initial appearances to the contrary, contemporary man's self-problematic nature is highly meaningful. But it takes a Christian philosophical perspective to appreciate most clearly how truly meaningful it is and how it can best contribute to man's self-creation.

PROBLEMATIC MAN

PART ONE

Problematic Man

THE problem towards whose solution I would here like to supply several elements is a problem in the second degree, a problem regarding a problem. I will formulate it in this way: Under which conditions has man become, in his entirety, a question for man?

It is important here to anticipate all misunderstanding, and I insist on the words which I have just used. It is obvious that for many centuries, and already in ancient Greece, man has asked himself questions which concerned now his origins, now his nature, now his destiny. But one can imagine, it seems to me, that these questions, as grave as they might be, stood out against the background of a certain assurance, or even of a certain obviousness. One could express this by saying that man's inner mirror reflected to him an image of himself in which he had no difficulty recognizing himself, an image which in itself was not at all disturbing.

But we are obliged to observe that at least at a certain level of knowledge, this is no longer so today: this level is that of interrogative reflection or thought. It is obvious, of course, that the immense majority of human beings never arrive at this level, or at best only ascend to it at rare moments favored by exceptional circumstances. But it is fitting to observe, on the other hand, that the attainment of this awareness, even if it is the feat of a small number, cannot help but have widespread repercussions and affect even those who did not seem to participate in it directly.

Let us observe, furthermore, that contemporary art, in certain of its most disconcerting expressions, constitutes an irrecusable

17

testimony of what must be called an alienation, taking the word in a much more general sense than that given to it in a Marxist perspective. By alienation I mean the fact that man seems to have become more and more a stranger to himself, to his own essence —to the point of calling this essence into question, of refusing it at the very least all original reality, as one has seen in the extreme expressions of contemporary existentialism. Everything is as if art, in a Picasso for example, came to manifest—I mean, to make manifest—the deformed and as it were unrecognizable image which the inner mirror reflects to us. For it is difficult seriously to admit that this deformation be obtained arbitrarily, that it be but the product of a deliberate and as it were perverse activity, or merely of what is sometimes called the "ludic" consciousness, that is, such as it is exercised in play and without any utilitarian preoccupation. It is far more plausible to admit that we are in the presence of a profound need, which is that of objectifying what I will designate by a term purposefully very vague, namely, existential modalities which are situated below the level of day-to-day consciousness.

I do not at all propose, however, to insist on the aesthetic aspect of what I am dealing with here; and if I refer to it, it is because it has the advantage of rendering this problem tangible.

I will take as the point of departure of my own reflections the remarkable analysis which opens the extremely important work of the contemporary German philosopher, Hans Zehrer, entitled *Man in this World*. It was published in Hamburg in 1948. One finds in it an extraordinarily lucid awareness of the situation of contemporary man. The author concentrates his attentions first of all on what he calls the barracks man.

This man is about forty-five. His hair is gray. One would be tempted to take a certain crease in his face for an ironic smile, but little by little one becomes aware that this crease must have another meaning, for it is immutable: it is appropriate to think rather of a sort of freezing of the traits. This man has possessed a family, a house with its furniture, land, a farm, animals. He had his parents, a wife, children; close friends lived in the neighborhood. He no longer possesses anything but what he is wearing. He works eight hours a day, perhaps repairing a road, he has enough to eat, the food is even good. When he is not too tired, he can find an extra job which will get him a supplement of food or a little tobacco. One cannot say that the collectivity has not taken care of him, and he himself would not say so. He speaks little, always slowly, with reserve. He speaks of what he formerly possessed, of his family, of his farm, and he thereby becomes again a human being *in the present,* whereas he was one *in the past;* he soon falls again into his stolid silence. But before he does so he has asked a question, always the same, and he certainly does not expect to obtain an answer: "Who am I?", he asks. "What am I living for, and what is the meaning of all this?"

The State cannot answer him. It only knows abstract concepts: employment, agrarian reform, etc. The same is true of society in general: what exists for it is aid to refugees, emergency relief, etc. Always abstractions. In the universe of the State and of society, this man no longer presents any living reality. He is a number on a filing-card, in a dossier which includes an infinity of others, each one with its number. Nonetheless, this man is not a number, he is a living being, an individual, and as such he speaks to us of a house, a very definite house, which was his; of his family, who were also individuals, of his animals, each one of which had a name. And it is to all this that this man refers when he asks his

19

question without an answer: "Who am I? What is the meaning of all this?" Will another man, he too an individual, be in a position to enlighten him? He can do his best to introduce our man into his own life, into his own universe, he can even share with him everything that he possesses. But this life and this universe are not interchangeable, and even that would not be an answer.

Strange thing, it is precisely because this other man knows who he is and what he is living for—that he cannot answer the question of the barracks man. He can only understand this question imperfectly, for he does not know what it is like to have lost one's country, one's home, all those whom one loves. And even if he had lost all that, he would find himself in the same situation, closer as a consequence; but it is probable that then, far from being able to answer it, he would ask the same question.

But the problem thereby takes on an acute character. It concerns not only this individual in particular, but all the men who live in the same barracks-room. The question is like a cloud which floats above the barracks, above the entire camp; but there are many other similar camps. It hangs over this entire country, upon a part of the world.

Nothing prepared our man to have to ask such a question. Once upon a time he knew who he was and why he existed, and when, warmed by his tale, he again becomes for several moments a living man, he knows once more. But the years go by. He is tormented, he is worn out by this question without an answer. That it arise before the obscure abyss of nothingness, before the absolute void, this is his destiny. A strange and incomprehensible power has stolen from him everything which constituted his home, everything which permitted him to take on form.

But this man is not there simply for himself, on his own account. He is also the last link of an historical development. He marks its ultimate possibility. For thirty years this question has been in the making for a whole continent, and soon for the entire planet.

Who is responsible for what has happened here? The answers are of two kinds. First, one can say that these events have come about by themselves, without man having anything to do with them; or else one can claim that it is the other man who is to blame. In the first case, man will have the duty of discovering the laws which control such a becoming, and adapt himself to them. In the second case, it will be necessary to call the culprit to account: but who is it? He wears a mask, an infinity of masks, that of nationalism, of race, or of national socialism, or of capitalism, or of socialism or communism.

Yet scientific knowledge has not been able to do anything to change what has come about; it has perhaps even made the conflicts still more acute. And the same is true of all these masks. One can, of course, invent a new theory, a new culprit: the number of those who have lost everything is too considerable for such inventions, let us say even such discoveries, to be able to satisfy them. How hollow or paltry all that appears in the presence of nothingness!

Why have I thought it necessary to reproduce in its broad lines this analysis which, at a superficial glance, seems to concern but an extreme case, that of the unfortunate whom one designates by a rather irritating euphemism as *displaced persons?* It is because in reality, in a situation like that of our world today, nihilism is contagious, and it is precisely upon this contagion that we have to concentrate our attention.

If I find myself really *in the presence* of the barracks man, if I see myself in the obligation of imagining as concretely as possible the conditions in which arise these tragic questions without answers: *Who am I? What am I living for?*, it is impossible that I not feel myself inwardly affected and even in the end addressed by such questions.

First of all, I can, or even must, represent to myself that this extreme outcome may be mine tomorrow. It is not difficult for me to evoke circumstances owing to which I would find myself tomorrow in a situation identical to that of the unfortunate, whose fate is for me at first sight an object of astonishment and scandal.

This is true at once in fact and by right. I say by right, for I have no reason to suppose that these men have deserved their destiny, and to think that I, on the contrary, am exempt of all reproach. If I am innocent, they are innocent like me; if they are criminal, I am also.

One can say, in short, that meaninglessness is spreading before our eyes. A strange inner mutation is thereby produced which takes on the aspect of a genuine uprooting. Entirely new questions are being asked, they insist upon being asked where one hitherto seemed to be in an order which contained its own justification; it is the very order to which the barracks man belonged in the days when he was still a living being, when he was in the present.

He for whom reflection has become a need, a primordial necessity, becomes aware of the precarious and contingent character of the conditions which constitute the very framework of his existence. The word "normal," which he once made use of in a way which now seems to him so imprudent, is emptied of its significance, —let us say at least in that it is suddenly, as it were, marked by a sign which makes it appear in a new and disturbing light.

That which I believed normal is decidedly not as normal as all that, it is perhaps only realized under cover of rather exceptional circumstances, which surely do not present the guarantees of absolute duration which we very naïvely believed were implied.

But what is singular is that from the moment when attention has concentrated with a sufficient force upon the barracks man, or upon the deportee—one would say that it is transformed into a permanent projector which illuminates in a new and very disturbing way other human situations which one admitted abstractly or in the mass because one had not taken the trouble to imagine them; let us say, for example, the situation of the proletariat in faraway countries like India, Iran, or Egypt, and so on, nearer and nearer, until we arrive at those who are at our gates, whose conditions of existence we have so long admitted without ever making the burdensome or even dangerous effort to imagine concretely what they might be.

Will we have at least the resources of taking refuge in a *passe-partout* interpretation such as Marxism? It is not difficult to understand the sort of psychological comfort which we experience, without any doubt, at settling into it. Not only will it provide us with at least an apparent explanation for the miserable condition in which the countless victims find themselves whose unbearable destiny has become tangible to us; not only will it permit us— very conveniently—to distribute human beings into two categories, that of the oppressors and that of the oppressed—but it will also put us in a position to confer upon ourselves something like a certificate of exemption by which we are assured that we are "on the right side." It is, of course, self-evident that what one can call Marxist adherence implies, in itself, nothing which resembles this pharisaism. But it is not effective, it is not respectable, unless it is translated by a concrete engagement, by a participation in a certain struggle.

But reflection, if it does not arbitrarily come to a stop, shows me rather quickly that such an interpretation is but a refuge, that it does not take into account what is in question, and that moreover, as we have had an inkling already, it implies—or invariably occasions—that substitution of the abstract for the concrete, of the filing-card for the individual, which is precisely the evil which we are becoming aware of.

Moreover, to come back to the situation of the barracks man—how does Marxism, or anything resembling it, permit one to face up to it? We observe, on the contrary, that it is in the name of Marxism, or at least of an interpretation of this doctrine—perhaps abusive, but which claims to be orthodox—that countless beings have been placed in conditions which strip them of all concrete reality.

It seems that, on the whole, a certain bleeding heart of the human being, of human existence, has been laid bare in our time, under conditions which render profoundly suspicious, for a lucid mind, any attempt to cover it up again, to dissimulate it. I have intentionally used this word, so imprecise in appearance: a certain heart. Indeed, it is not what one can call in all rigor an essence. In our perspective the problem of essence can appear to be, at least at first glance, secondary and almost insignificant. What is our reaction, for example, if one reminds us that man, in the words of Aristotle, is a rational animal? I do not think that it crosses our mind to say: *This formula is false,* for if one emphasizes the rapport between reason and articulate language, it cannot be seriously contested. Rather, what we will be tempted to say is that it seems to us to be *based* on a reality which we

24

are not sure it adheres to very closely; we could also say that it seems to us to be less significant than it was to our predecessors.

The profound justification of the philosophies of existence has perhaps consisted above all in the fact that they have brought out the impossibility of considering an existent being without taking into consideration his existence, his mode of existence. But regarding this very existence, the words *rational animal* furnish us no genuine enlightenment. At best one could here introduce the notion, current today, of *project,* and say that it enters into the project of the human being to behave as a rational animal. One could nevertheless wonder whether this notion is not ambiguous: it seems at first glance to present a psychological significance, but upon reflection this appearance dissipates. Psychologically, it is no doubt false to say that every human being has the project of behaving as a rational animal. Futhermore, we are perhaps justified in doubting the validity of a proposition which applies to every human being: perhaps by its very form it implies a negation of what is specifically human. Perhaps it substitutes—without the very one who expresses it being aware of the substitution —a certain nature, a certain complex, defined biologically, for that mysterious reality, the human being, of whom, after all, one could possibly only speak with propriety in the singular.

Moreover, the philosophies of existence which I have alluded to do not necessarily posit the priority of existence over essence. On the contrary Jean-Paul Sartre is today about the only one who feels obliged to make this affirmation. What these philosophies accentuate is the impossibility of contenting oneself with a traditional way of conceiving the rapports between essence and existence, and of admitting that existence, so to speak, comes to

25

superadd itself in an inexplicable or irrepresentable way to an essence which would be sufficient unto itself.

Let us now go back to the questions which the barracks man was asking himself: *Who am I? What sense does my life have?* It is obvious that one does not resolve these questions by saying to this man (or to myself if I ask them of myself): You are a rational animal. An answer of this kind is beside the point. I said earlier that meaninglessness was spreading: that is to say that I, who have a profession, a country, means of existence, etc., cannot help but turn these questions somehow towards myself. Why is this so? Let us reason *a contrario,* and suppose that I shut myself up prudently, jealously, in that favored category where these questions do not arise. But if I have really managed, by an effort of imagination, to put myself in the place of the barracks man, it is through his eyes that I will be brought to consider the step by which I placed myself once and for all in the category of the privileged, who know who they are, and what they are living for. In other words, by the combined action of imagination and reflection, I have been able to bring about a change which bears not only upon the object, but upon the subject himself, the subject who questions.

But in this new perspective, beginning with this new subjectivity, my way of taking my own conditions of existence for granted appears to be a mere impudence. In other words, I have become "detached" from these conditions which I spontaneously treated as self-evident, and the consequence of this detachment is that suddenly I too no longer know who I am. Let us observe, moreover—and this remark is extremely important—, that at the point where I have arrived, the question *Who am I?* has deepened to the point of addressing the very one who asks it. Who am

26

I, I who question regarding myself? Let no one come say that I thereby engage myself in an infinite regression. This regression would be vain, it would not change in the least the essential question.

But it is perhaps beginning with this point that there would be grounds for returning backwards, for going back towards the past, —in short, for asking oneself how this situation, which gives rise to this question and its own duplication, was created historically. One could thus, at this stage of reflection, ask oneself what historical events led to the transfers of population or the massive deportations which have resulted in the apparition of the barracks man. I will not stress this purely historical aspect of the problem. But one can certainly remark that there occurred in the nineteeth century a conjunction of nationalism on the one hand, and of the industrial revolution on the other, whose effects have been extremely harmful to man. One cannot even say that nationalism helped to render the yoke of industry more bearable; to the contrary.

But in reality one could not stop there. It would be necessary to investigate how nationalism and industrialism developed conjointly, and also what consequences they have had for the image which man has formed of himself and of the world in which he takes root.

In particular, one can hardly contest the fact that nationalism in its modern, post-revolutionary form is the product of an ideology that developed in the eighteenth century and combined, under conditions very difficult to state precisely, with a pre-romanticism whose origins seem to be found in Rousseau. Abandoned to its own inclination, this ideology led to a kind of cosmopolitanism of reason. The nationalism issued from the French

Revolution built itself to a large extent upon the ruins of the basic communities which had persisted until the end of the *ancien régime,* but which the individualism of the philosophy of the Enlightenment inevitably helped to dissolve. One cannot deny, on the other hand, that there was a close connection between this fact and the devitalization of religion which occurred in the same period. But the industrial revolution, at least during the first part of the nineteenth century, was destined to play a part in considerably aggravating this tendency—to a large extent, moreover, under the influence of a liberalism which on the economic plane (as we know all too well) was destined to engender the most inhuman consequences, the individual being reduced to a more and more fragmentary condition, under the cover of an optimism which seems to us today to have been the height of hypocrisy. But it is remarkable that Marxism itself, despite the differences between or even the opposition among its postulates, played a role in prolonging the liberal error; in other words, it did almost nothing to establish the advent of the person. Like liberalism, it remains in the end dependent upon the spirit of abstraction, and it is in this that it distinguishes itself so profoundly from Proudhonian socialism, which is profoundly respectful of the concrete.

These are but a few points of reference, but they are indispensable. It would still be necessary to show how what the great historian Ferrero called unleased wars were made possible; these wars were destined, for obvious reasons, to play a role in further weakening the sense of personal dignity and in paving the way quite paradoxically to a type of socialization which certainly no longer had anything to do with the generous thoughts which had animated the first socialist reformers in the middle of the nineteenth century.

But the essential is elsewhere, or more exactly, must be sought on a plane which is not that of the visible unfolding of events. I will dare to say, for my part, that the process which results in the barracks man and in the anxious questioning around which all these reflections gravitate, is a genuine necrosis whose principle is metaphysical.

In a general way, if we consider the historical and sociological evolution such as it has taken place for the past two cenutries, it seems that man has lost his divine reference: he ceases to confront a God as His creature and image. Might not the death of God, in the exact sense that Nietzsche has given to these words, be at the origin of the fact that man has become for himself a question without an answer?

It is no doubt fitting to state here, as precisely as possible, what one should understand by the expression "the death of God." It has been remarked that it is already found in an early work of Hegel, but in a context which does not permit one to attribute to it the precise sense which it will have for the author of *Zarathustra*. It is above all appropriate to refer to the famous passage in *Joyful Wisdom*, which is later developed in *Zarathustra*.

Have you ever heard of the madman who on a bright morning lighted a lantern and ran to the market-place calling out unceasingly: "I seek God! I seek God!" And as there were many people standing about who did not believe in God, he caused a great deal of amusement. Why! is he lost? said one. Has he strayed away like a child? said another. Or does he keep himself hidden? Is he afraid of us? Has he taken a sea-voyage? Has he emigrated? —the people cried out laughingly, all in a hubbub. The insane man jumped into their midst and transfixed them with his glances. "Where is God gone?" he called out. "I mean to tell you! *We have killed him,* —you and I! We are all his murderers! But how have we done it? How were we able to drink up the sea? Who gave us the sponge to wipe away the whole horizon? What did we do when we loosened this earth from its sun? Whither does it now move? Whither do we move? Away from all suns? Do we not dash on unceasingly? Backwards, sideways, forwards, in all directions? Is there still an above and below? Do we not stray, as through infinite nothingness? Does not empty space breathe upon us? Has it not become colder? Does not night come on continually, darker and darker? Shall we not have to light lanterns in the morning? Do we not hear the noise of the grave-diggers who are burying God? Do we smell the divine putrefication? —for even Gods putrefy! God is dead! God remains dead! And we have killed him! How shall we console ourselves, the most murderous of all murderers? The holiest and the mightiest that the world has hitherto possessed, has bled to death under our knife, —who will wipe the blood from us? With what water could we cleanse ourselves? What lustrums, what sacred games shall we have to devise? Is not the magnitude of this deed too great for us? Shall we not ourselves have to become Gods, merely to seem worthy of it? There never was a greater event, —and on account of it, all who are born after us belong to a higher history than any history hitherto!"

In Book V, written four years later, in 1886, Nietzsche expressed himself in the following way:

The most important of more recent events—that "God is dead," that the belief in the Christian God has become unworthy of belief—already begins to cast its first shadows over Europe. . . . In the main, however, one may say that the event itself is far too great, too remote, too much beyond most people's power of apprehension, for one to suppose that so much as the report of it could have *reached* them; not to speak of many who already knew *what* had taken place, and what must all collapse now that this belief had been undermined, —because so much was built upon it, so much rested on it, and had become one with it: for example, our entire European morality. This lengthy, vast and uninterrupted process of crumbling, destruction,

ruin and overthrow which is now imminent: who has realised it
sufficiently today to have to stand up as the teacher and herald of
such a tremendous logic of terror, as the prophet of gloom and
eclipse, the like of which has probably never taken place on earth
before? . . .

It is impossible to overemphasize the significance or the existential import of the Nietzschean formulas. Even though they have
a resonance which is no doubt personal, it is not exclusively subjective. It is an established fact that Nietzsche, in his youth, was
a believer, that God was then alive for him, but also that later
on he as it were withdrew from him. One has perhaps been right
to bring out the analogy between what happened there and the
tragic evolution of the rapports between Nietzsche and Wagner.
But it is absolutely characteristic of him that Nietzsche never
restricted himself to seeing therein an event of his personal life:
this eclipse, which he considered definitive, had for him a universal import, and in this sense one can legitimately speak of the
prophetism of Nietzsche.

But that is not all. Nietzsche, as we have seen, did not restrict
himself to saying "God is dead" in the sense in which Pascal,
recalling a passage of Plutarch, said, "The Great Pan is dead."
The Nietzschean affirmation is infinitely more tragic, since it
states that we ourselves have killed God, and it is this alone
which can account for the sacred dread with which Nietzsche
here expresses himself. I have been assured that Jean-Paul Sartre,
at the zenith of his renown, when he was welcomed by the
journalists at Geneva on the morrow of the Liberation, declared
to them straightway: "Gentlemen, God is dead." How could one
fail to see that the existential tone is absolutely different here,
precisely because the sacred dread has disappeared, and has been

31

replaced by the satisfaction of a man who claims to establish his doctrine upon the ruins of something in which he never believed? One can say, however, that already in Nietzsche the affirmation of the death of God presented a preliminary character, in the sense that this tragic event prepared the arrival of the superman, possibly only after the act by which man faces the death of God and acknowledges himself in some way responsible for it.

Heidegger, in the study which he devoted to the death of God in Nietzsche in *Die Holzwege,* recalls that with the consciousness of the death of God begins that of a radical transvaluation of the values until then considered as the highest. Man himself passes from that moment on into a different and higher history, because the will to power is there experienced and recognized as the principle of any ordering of values. It is thereby, moreover, and one cannot insist too much upon it, that Nietzsche claimed to transcend the nihilism which we would be reduced or condemned to if we stopped at the death of God, if we settled down in this tragic ascertainment, if we got from it a sort of perverse joy, instead of understanding that it can be but a point of departure, something like a trampoline for the prodigious leap, for the creative impulse without which the superman, the super humanity, is unthinkable.

One thus entirely misunderstands the profound intention of Nietzsche if one does not see in the forefront of his thought the will to overcome nihilism. For him, nihilism is linked to the decomposition of Christianity and perhaps still more generally of idealistic thought. For Nietzsche, as Jaspers has very well observed, nihilism derives from moral interpretation.

According to Nietzsche, nihilism derives from the claim to

apply to the world, in an absolute way, the categories of meaning and totality. It appears when, after having supposed in the entire event a totality and an organization such that the good of the whole would demand the self-sacrifice of the individual, one finally becomes aware that there is no whole at all. The idea of value would here not be able to survive the disparition of the whole, which conferred upon it an infinite character. Thus Nietzsche was able to say in *The Will to Power:* "The nihilist is the man who, regarding the world as it is, judges that it should not be, and regarding the world as it should be, judges that it does not exist: from then on, empirical reality has no meaning."

But the superman is precisely not a particular exemplar of the human species in whom the faculties of the ordinary man are deliberately increased; nor is he a species of man which would only arise through the application of the Nietzschean philosophy: he is the new man in his plenitude, whose humanity consists in the fact that in him the will to power becomes determinant in relation to reality.

It would be appropriate here, of course, to show that the will to power, considered as the innermost essence of being, seeks to realize on a higher plane what is already in life, to the extent that life is that which should always transcend itself. It is the very idea of transcending which is fundamental; so that being, which is will to power, dominates life, as something which it is always ready to abandon in order to be genuine. Under these conditions—and although the very expressions which Nietzsche often uses are unfortunately such as to facilitate this misinterpretation—it is without a doubt a very grave error to interpret the will to power in a purely biological sense. But one must acknowledge that what the doctrine thereby gains in depth, it loses in clarity. As for me, I would be rather inclined to think that Nietzsche, very strongly influenced at a certain period of his life by the thought of naturalists, and particularly by that of Darwin, was led to use a language, a notional equipment, originally borrowed from Schopenhauer and ulteriorly from the sciences of life, in order to translate a profound intention very difficultly reducible to that which this language could really convey. This disparity was destined, moreover, to bring about disastrous consequences historically, since the contemporary theoreticians of racism and Nazism, which are situated in reality at the opposite pole from Nietzchean thought, were nonetheless to call upon it, reproducing such or such a formula which, separated from its context, could seem to justify their monstrous enterprises.

Under these conditions one can think that Heidegger has to some extent grounds for claiming, in particular in his book *Discourse on Thinking,* that Nietzsche's thought is centered on a metaphysics—or rather, on an ontology—which he did not state explicitly.

All these questions are philosophically of the greatest importance. But on the terrain upon which I have placed myself, what it is in fact appropriate to acknowledge is that faith in the coming of the superman, such as it is expressed in particular in *Zarathustra,* has remained an almost exclusively Nietzschean datum; whereas the affirmation of the death of God has found in an infinity of minds a tragic and as it were definitive resonance. There is reason to reflect at length upon the reasons why this is so, as also upon the motives for which the idea of eternal recurrence, which represented for Nietzsche at the period of *Zarathustra* so eminent a value, constitutes for us today but an element, however significant, of his personal thematics.

However, what we have especially to observe here is that the transvaluation announced and demanded by Nietzsche not only has not taken place, but seems today to be as unrealizable as a monetary reform which an individual, even if he were a genius, were to claim to accomplish all by himself. Yet the most serious thing is that we have seen develop before our eyes a hideous caricature of this transvaluation itself, a caricature which, one can affirm without fear of error, would have been an object of indignation and horror for the author of *Zarathustra*. To be assured of this fact one has but to refer, for example, to the admirable Chapter IX of *Beyond Good and Evil,* which is entitled "What Is Noble?", in particular the paragraphs 250 and 251 which refer to the Jews.

From this moment on, Nietzsche's work appears to us marked, so to speak, by a genuine sign of contradiction, so that it can present itself simultaneously as infinitely dangerous and infinitely salutary; and this ambivalence, still more evident here than in Dostoevski, for example, corresponds to a general trait profoundly characteristic of our time.

Even the personal destiny of Nietzsche can be considered as significant, as symptomatic, although one must here be extremely prudent and circumspect. But in fact it seems rather difficult, when one fixes one's thought on Nietzsche's final shipwreck, to be content with accounting for it medically by a physiological taint, or a lesion, whatever it might be. It is certainly not a question of denying the doctor the right to proceed with the type of investigation, or even explanation, which is his; but in the presence of a great mind, who more than anyone else in his time contributed to the renewal of the intellectual horizon, a higher demand for intelligibility arises in us, to which the answers of science can provide no genuine satisfaction. How would one not be inclined to see in Nietzsche's madness the fatal and tragic manifestation of a spirit of disproportion which already attached itself in some way to the prophetism of Zarathustra, and to the very conception of the superman? It was perhaps impossible, after all, that he who dared to present himself as the announcer of the superman would not claim for himself some of the attributes of super humanity; and, under the weight of this claim, was it not normal that a frail human organism finally came to give way?

However this may be, it seems to me rather evident that at the present time it is above all the Nietzschean diagnosis, as well as his prognosis (to the extent that we can dissociate it from his prophetism, strictly speaking), which can and should be retained.

What has happened almost before our eyes is a gigantesque devaluation in many ways comparable to that which has taken place in so many countries on the monetary plane. This devaluation can be interpreted in various ways, according to whether one emphasizes the fact that certain values are no longer acknowledged at all, or the way in which they are disintegrating; that is to say, that they give rise to anarchic and incoherent interpretations.

Under these conditions it is altogether comprehensible that many philosophers arrive at the conclusion that, far from values being endowed with an independent reality, it is the self which creates them. One must add that the self meant here must be conceived in an empirical sense; we are at the opposite pole from the thought of a Fichte, which remained rigorously universalist— although experience has proved that it was susceptible of sliding dangerously towards nationalism, or even imperialism. But in the existential philosophies today, nothing of the sort is conceivable. They run the risk much rather of leading to anarchy, or else, in order to avoid losing themselves in it, they will tend to conclude the most hazardous of compromises with doctrines deriving from Hegel, and preferably with Marxism.

In reality, it is on the plane of values, as Nietzsche saw with depth, that we can best grasp what the death of God means. To the extent that God is identified with the super-sensible order in its entirety—I will add, for my part, inasmuch as He is ordered around an ineffable presence—, it will become impossible for us, for example, to speak of the Good in absolute terms, for the Good will appear inseparable from an existential decision which is realized under certain determined conditions.

But from what I have just said it follows that thought is here cornered, a ruinous dilemma is forced upon it: in a first hypothesis we are reduced to what I have called a pulverization, an atomization incompatible with the intention or the exigency implied in the very idea of the good. This atomization cannot help but engender a state of war to which only victory can put an end—quite temporary, moreover, for victory provokes the resentment of the conquered and thus prepares the upsetting, itself temporary, of what was but a *de facto* situation. But it is obvious that even from the point of view of history and sociology this idea of an atomized or pulverized good is indefensible, the good never being defined but in relation to a group, a collectivity. The problem thereby becomes singularly complicated, and we see the other branch of the dilemma appear, the society being here substituted for the self. But it is not by this angle either that we will be able to escape a ruinous relativism. Now history, provided that we consider it at a sufficient depth, teaches us that

37

the individual conscience, inasmuch as it is the bearer of universal values, can rise up against the collectivity and oppose a genuine justice—I mean, affirmed as genuine—to the false would-be justice which society intends to impose. It is evident that the whole problem is to know on what conditions we can confer a meaning and a value upon an opposition of this kind. The sociologist left to his own resources will be reduced either to contesting purely and simply the grounds for these distinctions, or else to declaring that this individual, be he Socrates or Christ, is but the percursor who anticipates an order which the society will ulteriorly establish. But there is nothing here which can be regarded even as the sketch of a solution, for one would still have to know upon what one intends to establish this hierarchy between the order which is that of a society called primitive, and that of the society of tomorrow. It is obviously not upon the simple temporal distinction between before and after that we can establish anything which resembles a value judgment. We can only get out of this inextricable situation by declaring that the prophetic individual is the bearer of a certain message which translates a transcendent truth. This word *transcendent* has here a principally negative signification which it is important to bring to light. We mean that the value here in question can only be recognized or acclaimed by a regard which is not oriented along a purely temporal axis, along a line linking simply a before and an after. One could escape the necessity of introducing this dimension, which the word "transcendent" expresses after a fashion, only by laying down as a principle that evolution is by itself a progress. But one must answer not only that this is a postulate to which experience and history oppose a categorical refutation, since undeniable decadence and deteriorations exist, but also—

and as a consequence—that one will inevitaby be under the obligation of sorting out the phenomena or the events which succeed one another in order to see where this progress is situated. But how could this very sorting out be accomplished if not by recourse to one or more criteria which are themselves transcendent in the sense that I have defined? From this moment on it seems that there is no mean: one will either waive all evaluation to shut oneself up in a radical subjectivism, but there can then no longer be a question of progress in any sense—or else one will maintain a value judgment, but this will only be possible by calling in the other dimension.

It is in this perspective that one should reconsider the situation from which we started, that of the barracks man, as well as the power of contamination with which, we have seen, it is almost inevitably endowed.

It is quite certain—and I have taken care to emphasize it—that man, reduced to a destitution such that his life has become meaningless for him, preserves the memory of a different life which still presented a character of plenitude. It is then a question of knowing what appraisal it is possible to make of this other life, of this other world, on the basis of a situation which is that of a being entirely dispossessed. There are grounds for wondering whether this experience of nothingness—for we can indeed thus designate it, *groso modo*—is not going to corrode retrospectively, like an acid, the memory of this happy past. This can seem absurd at first: for in the last analysis, one can say, this memory is what it is and should not be able to be affected by the present, whatever it may be. But it is to be feared lest this objection be based on the completely illusory notion that memory is assimilable to a somehow objective effigy, which we preserve

39

as we preserve an album of photographs in a drawer. But memory is something else, it is a certain way of reliving a previous experience, one could say that it is an experience of the second degree, and if this is so, the contamination of the past by the present becomes possible and perhaps inevitable. As so often, it is the images borrowed from the theory of light which are the most pregnant here: that plenitude which characterized the past experience is in danger of appearing now in such a light that it appears ridiculous. This is about what would happen for a man who, discovering that his wife or his friend has just deceived him, were to evoke the intimacy in which he lived of late with the one or the other: it would be as if this intimacy in which he believed had suddenly become grimacing. One can nevertheless answer that it is unjust, and perhaps absurd, to make the ulterior event affect in this way a phase of life which, taken in itself, presented a positive value. But it is precisely a question of knowing whether something very profound in us does not refuse this sort of fragmentation where it is a question of human beings, of being. This is true in the general situation upon which the whole of this inquiry bears, as well as in the particular example which I have chosen as a point of comparison. What I have called intimacy did not amount to the simple ascertainment of an agreeable state: it involved an expectation, a confidence in a future which would come to confirm and even no doubt deepen the present experience. Now, it is precisely this expectation which has been betrayed. From this moment on, the intimacy itself appears as having been illusory.

But in reality, almost the same thing is true for him who believed himself established in a certain mode of existence in which everything seemed to ring true. Here too, a certain confidence, perhaps implicit, perhaps inarticulate, has been betrayed, but not by anyone in particular: by something which one does not really know what to call, and which seems to be the very element in which one exists. It is evident, moreover, that this preposition "in" translates very inexactly a relation infinitely more intimate, and perfectly comparable to that which links the living being to the atmosphere which it needs in order to breathe, that is, to an element which not only surrounds it, but penetrates it. Now it is this element, almost impossible to designate, which suddenly presents itself as betrayal; and all the more as it was precisely in this element that the man had placed that confidence, itself defying formulation, but which seemed to be one with life itself. However, one must not hesitate to say that nihilism, inasmuch as it is lived, as it does not amount to a simple theoretical affirmation, always appears as the prolongation or the development of this elementary discovery, which one could also describe as something like a convulsion: the unity which one believed indissoluble between life and the confidence in life was illusory. From this moment on, the same holds true for values, for as I have already given to understand, values were ordered around the ineffable feeling of this unity.

It would perhaps also be fitting to express oneself here with more rigor and to say that as soon as values allow themselves to be dissociated from this central affirmation, they break up, and at the same time each of them seems to lose its vitality, to be reduced to its own skeleton, that is, in short, to something which one recognizes as a mere idea. In other words, the value no longer adheres to the reality, whatever be the genuine nature of the latter.

Nihilism should thus be seen as the end of a process of decomposition which takes place from the moment when, in one way or another, the original plenitude of past experience has fallen apart; and we should think here of withering and death, for it is therein that we find the most visible, the most significant expression of this process. There are grounds, moreover, for showing, in a perspective which is not very different from that of Nietzsche, that many solutions, many landings at which the mind has paused, particularly in the idealist philosophies, are as it were stages on a road which leads to nihilism.

But it is here essential to make an observation of fundamental importance: a genuinely spiritual process cannot truly be assimilated to that which unfolds on the plane of organic life, for it implicates freedom; it is freedom, and it alone, which intervenes in the very act which would consist in denying it.

Let us take up our examples again, and first of all the one which has served us as an illustration, namely, a man betrayed by his wife or by his friend. If I identify myself in thought with this man, my reflection can orient itself in the following way: it is true that what seems to me retrospectively like my previous happiness involved an implicit expectation, and it is also true that this expectation has been disappointed. But does it follow from this that everything was delusion in the experience which was mine? I cannot affirm it except by a free decision made in this very moment in which I am, and this decision made in the direction of negation or of nothingness could well constitute an act of infidelity or ingratitude, since it amounts to declaring null a gift nonetheless real. Since in any case I must decide, would not the truth be rather in the act by which I would acknowledge the reality of this gift, and would even emphasize this reality, and not the conditions, as painful as they may be, in which it has been withdrawn, —that is, in this case, the withering which has taken place in the being whom I loved. This applies still more directly to the so frequent case in which we revolt against destiny which has prematurely taken a loved one from us, thus striking with a sort of retrospective malediction the happiness which this person had given us. Here, in the most distinct possible way, we see that it is for us to decide for or against being; and this certainly means that in one case we affirm the primacy of being, and in the other that of nothingness.

One will perhaps be inclined to observe, it is true, that this supposed decision consists only in words which in no way change the substance of things. But as a matter of fact, this is false: for what counts is not the words, it is the inner attitude of which these words are only the sign or the symbol. By affirming the primacy of nothingness, I fall back upon my despair, I close myself up inwardly; and to the extent that it is possible for me, I enclose the others in this sort of prison, whereas it is the inverse if I proclaim that what should count above all is that participation in what is best which has been accorded to me, be it for a very short time.

But in this second case, something strange can take place, which I could not pay too much attention to. It *can take place*, I have said: for obvious reasons it could not indeed be a question here of an inevitable or mechanical development. This participation in what is best can appear to me as something which I cannot truly say is simply in the past. Let us note in passing the extremely significant analogy between the idea which we said *was a mere idea* and a past which one would say is but the past. I can be led to discover that from the moment that I give evidence of fidelity by proclaiming the infinite value of this participation, no matter what may have happened later, it is as if a current which had seemed interrupted were reëstablished, as if a spring which appeared dried up began to flow again; as if the deprivation which was and remains so cruel for me lost its definitive character, as if what I have lost were somehow given back to me. I will attempt to express this by saying that if I manage to adopt the inner attitude which corresponds to the affirmation of the primacy of being, I give grace its chance, that is, I put myself in position to receive it, without, of course, having the pretension of setting it in motion—which would have no sense unless it were a natural or physical power.

But let us not fail to observe that everything which has just been said concerns being, not those values separated from being which I said marked out the road which leads to nihilism.

Now, this could well be of the greatest importance for the problem which has not ceased to occupy us from the beginning.

To say that the Self creates values is to distort in the most dangerous way a much more profound truth, which concerns not only freedom but the significance which is immanent in it, and that to such an extent that if one deprives it of this significance, freedom is transformed into an absurd and grimacing caricature of itself.

The truth is much rather that if the Self intervenes, it is as a factor of decomposition of being considered in its plenitude, or, to borrow the language of Simone Weil, as a principle of de-creation. If the Self is at the origin of values, it is inasfar as the latter, as I have indicated and as Heidegger has perfectly stated, correspond to a minus-being, that is, to a reduction carried out upon being. This reduction is, moreover, the preliminary condition of an action whatever it be, inasfar as this action presupposes

44

a project. One could say that the value is, so to speak, the horizon against which this project, this action, is outlined. One can also say that it is the schematic interpretation which the consciousness gives itself of the enterprise it engages in by throwing itself into action. But one must recognize at the same time—as André Gide saw towards the debut of his career, without, however, following this observation to its final implications—that all action, in as far as it is a choice, is a mutilation, and one could even say an insult to the real. The human tragedy consists in part in the fact that each one of us is condemned to this mutilation, for he becomes himself only on this condition, but also in the fact that he is obliged to redeem this fault, if it is one, by a sort of compensatory action, which consists in fact in the restoration of the unity which he has helped to shatter by his choice. One can ask oneself whether this compensatory value would not confer the most profound meaning upon the religious act such as it is accomplished in prayer or meditation, but also in the poet or the artist. Formulas at first very disconcerting, like that of Heidegger defining man as *the shepherd of being,* here take on a profound meaning. I would like to attempt to elucidate it here a little, without worrying too much about whether my thought coincides perfectly with that of the German philosopher; indeed, I will take care not to adopt his terminology, which is moreover very difficult to transpose into another language.

To say that man is the shepherd of being is to attribute to him a certain ontological responsibility. But this would have no meaning, strictly speaking, if being were conceived as endowed with an existence in itself, in the same way as nature, such at least as we are accustomed to conceive of it. On the other hand, it could not be a question—still in order that the formula have

45

a meaning—of reducing being to modalities of the thinking subject, after the fashion of a certain idealism. It is thus necessary
to follow a narrow channel between two opposing conceptions,
which must both be set aside. The extreme difficulty of the latest
philosophy of Heidegger derives to a great extent precisely from
the fact that he attempts to navigate between reefs, and it seems
that language somehow denies him its services. This is all the
more paradoxical because no one has shown more forcibly than
he that there is a sort of original sanctity of language. "Language," he wrote at the beginning of his *Letter on Humanism,*
"is the home of being, it is in it that man establishes his abode.
The thinker and the poet are the guardians of this habitation."
But one must certainly add that language has not been able to
conserve its original purity, and that it tends to transform itself
before our eyes into a system of signs whose value is purely instrumental and technical. This explains Heidegger's constant
effort to connect himself either to poets such as Hölderlin or to
the pre-Socratic philosophers who were at the same time poets,
such as Anaximander, Parmenides, or Heraclitus. The danger
here is that he proceeds much too often to an arbitrary recon-
struction on the basis of his own intentions, instead of asking
himself what these thinkers actually meant. Yet is is difficult to
blame him in principle. Max Picard, too, distinguishes between
speech and the kind of inarticulate, confused noise, *Wortge-
räusch,* to which it is reduced among contemporary barbarians.
One could say that speech is exposed to a double peril, either as
it becomes algebraic (in particular by the abuse of initials and by
the vocables obtained by juxtaposing them: U.N., N.A.T.O.,
etc.), or as it is degraded into a slovenliness which resembles
expectoration.

The genuine problem would be to know what the relation is between speech pronounced in its truth, in its rigor—and being, strictly speaking. It would here be necessary to reflect very profoundly upon the essence of naming. At first, it would seem that it consists simply in the choice of a conventional sign destined to serve as a substitute for the thing designated. One can obviously not say that this is false, but this exclusively functional interpretation seems still to overlook the essential, precisely insofar as this essential cannot be functionalized. It may be interesting to refer to the—alas!—more and more frequent cases in which a human being is designated by a serial number: I have in mind here not only the prison, but the hospital, and even the large hotel. In all these cases there is elimination of that unfunctionalizable residue which becomes so mysteriously and so certainly present when one gives a name to a newborn child. But what is remarkable is that our thought tends to move in the functional domain to such an extent that it has the greatest difficulty coping with this sort of intimate core of naming. And nevertheless, it is manifest that we are here at the common root of a certain magic and of all poetry. If, then, we have said with Heidegger that man is the shepherd of being, it is evident that this formula cannot be interpreted in a functional sense either. It would be of the ultimate absurdity to say that the function of man is to guard being as one guards a flock, and if I have spoken of responsibilities, it is in a sense which is itself supra-functional, the sense in which I am responsible for my own children. We can refer here to the subtle difference which separates this responsibility from that incumbent on the nurse whom I entrust them to. If one places oneself on the terrain of *function* as such, this difference is perhaps not perceptible, but from the spiritual point of view it is evident: in the fact

47

that my child is genuinely consubstantial with me, which could not be the case for the nurse. The experience of contemporary life shows us, it is true, that everything is considered more and more according to the category of function, and it is thus that one has been able to see such and such a politician clamor for a remuneration for mothers of a family. The fact that the intrinsic absurdity of such a proposition could fail to be recognized immediately and without the least explanation clearly shows that the sense of being is in the process of disappearing.

These various examples illuminate one another. If now we come back to the problem of naming where it concerns an individual being, we will discover that it can only be really understood in a supra-functional sense as an act of love. To choose a name for my child is not at all merely or even essentially to establish a certain convention: it is truly a way of conferring his identity upon him, and affixing a certain seal upon the very act of paternity. Furthermore, one understands perfectly well why for so long and in so many countries the child has been placed by the very name given to him under the protection of a saint or an ancestor. His identity thereby lost any arbitrary or simply formal character. In the most profound sense of the word, the act of naming had a religious value or import; it was a consecration. But in a world in which the sense of universal communion, despite certain deceptive appearances, is in the process of disappearing, the name will be given under the influence of pure fantasy—which amounts to saying that it loses its supra-individual resonance. Thus we see that naming, metaphysical in its principle, can degenerate either by becoming functionalized or by being reduced to the expression of a caprice.

But I would be tempted to wonder whether such remarks do

not project a certain clarity upon the mystery of language in general. Let us not risk formulating some hypothesis or other regarding the origin of language; let us be content with noting that the problem of the origin appears more and more obscure, that it merges with that of the apparition of the human being—some will say of *hominisation*—, but that in any case, the naturalistic pseudo-explanations here reveal their radical insufficiency. What is important is much rather to bear in mind the conquest of language such as it takes place in every child: it is clear that in theory it can be accomplished only in the warmth of a home, and that on the other hand it is realized only in a kind of continuous wonder at things. One conceives all too easily what language becomes in a person who is not loved, who lives among human dregs and risks becoming himself a human reject. There thus appears, at once directly and *a contrario,* the relationship—so intimate that we can scarcely conceive it—between the blossoming of language and the conditions, human or otherwise, in which this blossoming is realized. Human or otherwise, —this means: penetrated with love or not. To the extent that he learns to speak, where these conditions are positive the child participates in a kind of re-creation of the world. But, as I have many times had the occasion to repeat, to create is never to produce; we are not going to drift into the absurdities of subjective idealism. If the child re-creates the world, it is in a sense far more intimate and more difficult to express, inasmuch as the world becomes for him a home. It is, in fact, a question here of a double incorporation. For one can say at the same time that the child treats the world more and more as a prolongation of his own body, but also that he comes to consider himself in a certain way as the body of a world which is his soul, and here one must apply oneself to un-

49

derstanding the mysterious office which reverie fills in the growth of the child.

One begins perhaps to catch a confused glimpse of how these thoughts, at once difficult and yet so close to what is most intimate and most ardent in the experience of formation, permit us to orient ourselves in regard to the question initially asked, that which arose in the barracks man.

This man appears, in short, to correspond to the extreme situation of a person placed in conditions dehumanizing to the point that his own humanity seems to him to be almost detached from himself, floating like a dream in which one almost no longer believes, but which nonetheless awakens in the soul an invincible nostalgia. The truth is that the barracks man is the victim of a crime without name, but which has something particularly atrocious about it: it can no longer be imputed to anyone in particular. We rediscover here, of course, the themes prophetically treated by Kafka in his novels and stories. But one must state that the anonymity in the crime does not suppress the crime, it merely denounces its metaphysical character. The most fatal error which we could commit would be to imagine that this anonymity is the sign of an historical necessity in the name of which the crime could or ought to be absolved. Now here, the intellectual of today is exposed to a temptation which must be mercilessly denounced by the philosopher. One of the most dangerous sorts of convergences is on the point of being established between an essentially Marxist philosophy of history and an existentialism centered on nothingness, or on the process of annihilation (*néantisation*) which defines the human condition beginning from the act, in itself unintelligible and unjustifiable, by which man is thrown into the world (*Geworfenheit*). Let us recall what Sartre says in *Being and Nothingness* of human reality: "For human reality, to be is to choose oneself: nothing comes to it from without, nor from within, that it can receive or accept. It is entirely abandoned, without any help of any sort, to the unbearable necessity of making itself be, down to the least detail. Thus freedom is not a being: it is the being of man, that is, his nothingness of being."

It is in this same perspective that Sartre, at the conclusion of his great work, declares that we must renounce the spirit of seriousness, which, he says, "has the double characteristic of considering values as transcendent givens, independent of human subjectivity, and of transferring the 'desirable' character of the ontological structure of things to their simple material constitution. For the spirit of seriousness, indeed, bread is desirable because one must live (a value written in the intelligible heaven) and because it is nourishing . . . Man blindly seeks being, hiding from himself the free project which is this search, he makes himself such as he is expected by the tasks placed on his path. Objects are silent demands, and he is nothing in himself but passive obedience to these demands."

But what is opposed here to the spirit of seriousness if not an exaltation of human freedom on the basis of the affirmation of an absolute void which is, as it were, its counterpart?

Logically, such a position implies an absolute anarchism, for it is impossible to see upon what principles one could base a hierarchy of values or of modes of expression of freedom. How would one not sacrifice anew to the spirit of seriousness by establishing this hierarchy? It is nonetheless a fact, a fact which singularly deserves to retain our attention, that since the publication of *Being and Nothingness* in 1943, and despite the very pertinent

51

criticism to which he himself submitted dialectical materialism a little later, Sartre has in fact not ceased drawing nearer to the Marxists, and, without yet affiliating himself with the Communist party, rising up against any anti-Communism of any kind. This evolution, which should logically appear completely unjustifiable, can probably be explained from the point of view of an existential psychoanalysis which lays bare the profound intentions, the initial project of the author. One can scarcely help recognizing that the spirit of seriousness which the author of *Being and Nothingness* attacks merges for him in a certain way —very arbitrarily, moreover—with the bourgeois spirit, as if a certain class had a monopoly on the idealism against which he rages. Let us not fail to remark, furthermore, that the word *idealism* is here as almost always rather deceptive, since it is in fact a question of belief in the instrinsic reality of values, so that *this* idealism could just as well be called a realism. But is not a rather different realism implied in Marxism as well? It is difficult to see how Marxism could in any way identify itself with a philosophy of freedom of the Sartrean type. If there is a common denominator, it is atheism, and one can wonder whether this is not, at least in part, the reason for which Marxism exercises such a force of attraction upon Sartre.

It seems to me that one can draw several conclusions from the preceding reflections, providing that one considers them as a whole.

The first, and perhaps the most important, could be formulated in the following way.

It is not in our power, it is no longer even among our possibilities, to retrograde towards the stage in history in which man could appear to himself as an evident given. And this strictly problematic character which man is obliged from now on to acknowledge to himself goes beyond the particular questions which arise in the perspective of specialized disciplines, such as paleontology, biology, even scientific anthropology. I would be strongly inclined to express myself here as I have regarding technology: it is an illusion, I said, to imagine that man, frightened by the consequences which the development of technology can engender, should forbid himself the use of the powers whose formidable character he has recognized. Technology is something which he is obliged from now on to bear, to assume under pain of denying himself. It is not a burden which he can set down in order to lighten his step. The same is true, on a very different plane, concerning the anguishing problem which arises for him as soon as he has ceased taking himself for granted. But it could be, after all, that this is the profound meaning of Nietzsche's discovery, or more precisely, of the awareness to which he came. It is perhaps not illegitimate to think that what is dead, what is out of date, is a certain manner of conceiving either God Himself, or, to speak more precisely, the specific mode of relation which unites me to this God to which I as man refer. The mode of relation, I have said; but I do not thereby refer to all relation, all reference, whatever it might be.

For a second conclusion to which our inquiry seems to lead is that man, from the moment he undertakes to set himself up as an absolute—that is to say, precisely, to free himself from all relation, from all reference to another than himself—can in the last analysis but destroy himself, or else—which amounts in the end to the same thing—emerge into an idolatry which takes an abstraction such as class or race as its object, that is, something incomparably inferior to the very thing from which he meant to break away.

But there seems thereby to open up before us an arduous inquiry which concerns the conditions under which this reference of man to another than himself, to a greater than himself, can be maintained without thought falling back, for all that, into the errors from which, by reflection, it has undertaken for centuries to liberate itself. In what follows, I can but limit myself to a few indications of which I recognize the complete insufficiency, but which will at least give a glimpse of the direction which should be followed, in my opinion, by a philosophy courageous enough not to let itself be intimidated by any of the dogmatics which confront one another today, as much on the side of atheism as on that of a theology still dependent upon traditional categories. And I ask myself not without astonishment whether it is not after all in the prolongation not only of Plato but of Kant that this course should be sought—on the condition, of course, above all as far as the latter is concerned, of dropping the letter of the doctrine: and I have in mind here formalism in all its aspects, particularly the ethical aspect.

To proceed immediately to what appears to me to be the essential, I think we should have done with the idea of a God as Cause, of a god concentrating in himself all causality, or even, in more rigorous terms, with all theological usage of the notion of causality. It is precisely here that Kant has shown us the way, perhaps without himself proceeding to the final consequences of his discovery. It could be, I will say in order to resume the thread of my argumentation, that the God whose death Nietzsche truthfully announced was the god of the Aristotelian-Thomistic tradition, god the prime mover. But in this line of thought, what is the significance of the fact that man has become once and for all a question for himself? Let us see first what this does not signify. As I have already said, it would be contrary to all reason to confer upon man anything resembling aseity, the fact of being his own cause, which is a pure absurdity. It means rather that if we claim to make of the idea of cause a transcendent use, we arrive at a dead-end, or, which amounts to the same thing, we get lost in a labyrinth. The words "transcendent use" have here an extremely precise meaning: they mean a use which extends beyond the domain of instrumentality strictly speaking—that is, that in which man exercises his mastery—or even any other domain conceived, arbitrarily or not, as analogous to the first. But man, the principle of instruments, can no doubt not think of himself as the product of transcendental instrumental action. If he is a question for himself, it is perhaps above all to the extent that it belongs to him to recognize that it is he as agent who is at the center of any causal representation. It is to be feared, indeed, that the idea of causality, whatever effort modern philosophers may have made to spiritualize it, to unfetter it, to detach it from its primitive anchors, is inseparable from the existence of a being provided with instrumental powers: it is, in short, bio-teleological.

But from this point of view the calling into question of man by himself appears in a new aspect. To be convinced of it, it is fitting to proceed to the interiorization, that is, to the transposition to the plane of reflection, of a problem which we are at first tempted to pose in an objective language. Inasfar as I treat myself as a thing, I cannot dispense myself from proceeding to an inquiry concerning the determinisms which have contributed to the production of this thing. But the idealist philosophies since Kant have been in agreement in showing that I cannot, without betrayal, identify myself with this thing, or even with a thing of any kind. And on this point, even a philosophy whose orientation is different must accord them its adhesion. It will merely have to beware of the other error, which is precisely that to which idealism has generally succumbed, and which consists in treating as an absolute this self, of which one has previously established that it cannot be assimilated to a thing and consequently cannot lend itself to the type of research or inquiry which bears upon things.

But, one will say, is not refusing to treat the individual subject as an absolute inevitably to integrate it into a new system which would itself be in some way deified, or of which, at the very least, God himself would be the center? Precisely here is situated the crucial point of our entire inquiry: in as far as I treat myself as a question, I must refuse this solution which can but be illusory, without falling back for all that into the error of a subjective idealism. Invocation, or prayer, which is the only living relation of the soul to God, is indeed only possible, it can only find its authentic locus, in the narrow channel which separates these errors, each of which must be judged mortal from the religious point of view: the one leading to a fatalism which destroys freedom, the other to solipsism and delirium.

Nonetheless, one will no doubt ask, is not my prayer addressed fundamentally to him whom I call my creator? But one must no doubt answer that we have to make an indispensable distinction between the act of creating and the act of producing. To think of oneself as produced would be anew to think of oneself as a thing. The most profound Christian thought has always affirmed that God has created me free: but this is only true as far as he himself has assigned a limit to his power of production. And it is precisely upon this limitation—and not upon this power—that I must fix my regard from the moment I concentrate my attention upon my being and upon the metaphysical conditions of its possibility. But if I am not taken in by the words, I must recognize that I do not conceive anything positive here, any positive conception no doubt implying an attempt at imaginative reproduction. I limit myself in reality to circumscribing a sort of space or void in which I discover or I decide that I have my being. It will not be up to my knowledge to fill this void, but rather to my action, to what I call my life. Just as a certain quality of atmosphere is required in order for breathing to be possible—and if I do not breathe, I die—, so too we discern here the spiritual element for want of which our existence denies itself. But the comparison is to some extent deceptive, for the atmosphere is still objectively definable, it remains a datum accessible, if not to our senses, at least to instruments which come to fill the lacunae of sensible experience. Here, on the contrary, all objective determination must be regarded as impossible or as self-destructive, and our fundamental situation implies that this should be so.

It is moreover all too clear that these terms of space and void should not be taken literally. Everything is in short as if, by an operation of whose aim we can have but an inkling, but in no way conceive the nature, a higher power without common measure with what we are, had, by a voluntary and partial limitation of itself, allotted to each living being its own terrain of development. Here again let us not fail to recall that such a way of presenting things is entirely inadequate, in as far as it seems to imply the purely spatial idea of a territory which would be divided up among a certain number of beneficiaries—that is, the idea of a land registry. One could say that the movement of religious consciousness, like that of philosophical reflection, consists precisely in liberating itself progressively from this representation, and in orienting itself on different levels towards the purely spiritual affirmation that each of us must recognize or rediscover himself in all the others, without for that losing anything of what constitutes his intimate originality.

In any case, without of course being able to give a figuration of any kind of it, we have to conceive of something like a locus where the encounter of freedom and grace becomes possible. In such a perspective, the idea of grace must be considered fundamental, and I will even be inclined to say that it is only on the basis of it that we can rise, as awkwardly as it may be, to the affirmation, I will not say of the existence, but of the presence of God. But the almost insurmountable difficulty which we encounter comes from the fact that, if we do not content ourselves with the overly abstract and at times verbal determinations with which the theologian has so often been satisfied in the past, we are almost inevitably exposed to the temptation to naturalize grace, that is, to interpret it as a force or as a supplement of force emanating from some mysterious center, identified with the divine power or will. If we have to be rigorous, as I have said, in the refusal of objectification, it is because in order to safeguard what one can call the very holiness of God, we have precisely to forbid ourselves all figuration of this kind. To be sure, on a subject of this kind philosophy and theology themselves can but stammer, theology having the advantage over philosophy of referring directly to the evidence which God has given of himself in Revelation. But one can admit, on the other hand, that until a relatively recent period theology has too often borrowed its conceptual equipment from philosophies which in their principle were not at all attuned to the demands of religious consciousness, and were bound, moreover, to an epistemology and a cosmology which are today outmoded. One of the most important tasks which can be assigned in our time to philosophy consists precisely, I am convinced, in reforging catagories which harmonize more directly with these very demands. And when I speak here of philosophy, I am obviously thinking in the first instance of ontology. I rejoin here what I indicated previously: if we can somehow, let us not say conceive an idea of grace, but orient ourselves towards that which, in conditions of experience different than ours, would become such an idea, it seems indeed that it is by regarding it as an afflux of being. But in order for *these* words to take on a concrete significance, we have, I think, to turn to the method of concrete approach which I attempted to define more than twenty years ago. These concrete approaches are situated in the perspective of what I have since called "inter-subjectivity." There is perhaps no one, even outside of all religious practice, nay, of all precise religious conviction, who has not had the direct experience of this afflux of being which can emanate for each of us from a word heard, sometimes even from a smile or a gesture. We are here beyond all psychology, for this word or this gesture are essentially bearers of something else, which can certainly not be contained in a formula or a concept. What is significant here is that he who has addressed this word or smile to us appears to us, without intending to or without even being aware of it, as the witness of a certain transcendent reality. It is obvious, on the other hand, that this recognition can be, as far as we are concerned, as inarticulate as possible and that this transcendent reality not only can be undesignated, but even remains most often at the stage of a background sensation. If I have repeatedly emphasized the fact of the *encounter* considered as vested with spiritual value impossible to overestimate, it is because this fact is situated in exactly the same perspective, it possesses an ontological sign, which amounts to saying that no psychological analysis enables one to exhaust its significance.

Contrary to the tendency which prevails nowadays among many philosophers unacquainted with any religious experience, I will even say with any religious concern, I remain convinced that it is only in relation to grace that human freedom can be defined in depth; and that if it is considered in itself, it is in great danger of changing into its opposite, or else of being reduced to a sort of ridiculous and caricatural analogy of the attributes of which one has beforehand divested a God considered nonexistent. In other words, freedom is no doubt essentially the acceptance or refusal which it is up to us to mark in relation to grace—this refusal, moreover, always being able to disguise itself in a fallacious neutrality. The important thing is simply to recognize that freedom cannot any more than grace be translated into a language of causality. Here again, new categories must be established, and it is Bergson who has paved the way.

It may seem that in the developments which have occupied a large part of this inquiry I have strayed from my initial subject. I believe, nonetheless, that this is not the case, for it is on the basis of the calling into question of man by himself, or of what some call interrogative thought, and only on that basis that reflection has a chance of progressing in the direction which I have just indicated. It is in this spirit, furthermore, in opposition to those who have artificially attempted to integrate me into what they call existentialism, that I have declared that the term neo-Socratism seemed to be much more appropriate for the at times stumbling gait which has been mine since I began to think by myself. Interrogative thought is opposed in the last analysis to everything which presents itself as assertion or, to use an English term which has no equivalent in French, as *statement*.[1] The distinctive feature of the *statement* is to be or to aim to be unanswerable; it presents a character of finality, and this is true for a very wide range of propositions, from "two and two make four" to an affirmation such as "Napoleon died at Saint Helena," despite the profound differences of modality which separate such propositions. One could easily show, moreover, that even a hypothetical proposition of the type: if it is true that A is B, it is also true that C is D, also presents itself as a *statement*. But what I have called the calling into question of man by himself presents the singular character of not emerging *into a possible statement*. Or perhaps it would be better to say that this calling into question extends at the same time to any *statement* bearing upon the origins, the essence or the very destiny of man. I believe it necessary, furthermore, to take great care not to confuse such a position with the agnosticism which prevailed in the nineteenth century, in Spencer for example. In fact this agnosticism, at least in England, seems to me to have remained dependent upon the idea developed by Hamilton that, since knowledge can only consist in the act of establishing relationships between given elements, the absolute being who is beyond all relationship necessarily escapes its grasps and remains as it were by definition unknowable. But critical and above all Hegelian idealism has shown once and for all that this implies an abstract notion of the absolute being to which it is impossible to accord an ultimate value. The line of thought which is mine is absolutely different.

1. [The italicized words in this paragraph are in English in the original text. —Tr.]

The critical point appears to me to be the following: a being whose most profound originality consists perhaps not only in questioning the nature of things, but in interrogating himself regarding his own essence, is situated by this very fact beyond all the inevitably partial answers to which this interrogation can lead. It is thus probably absurd to expect from prehistory a complete and definitive answer to the question of the origins of man, or from a scientific cosmology whatever it be, a solution to the problem of his nature. It is by no means a question of contesting the value of the results obtained by the particular disciplines. We have merely to acknowledge that if we know more and more things about man, we are perhaps less and less clear regarding his essence: I would even be disposed to wonder whether this profusion of partial knowledge is not after all blinding. I mean by this that it seems rather to exclude the possibility of that one simple answer, that is, in short, of that light to which something in us invincibly aspires. But what one must add is that by the very fact of this growth or this proliferation of positive science, it is the legitimacy of this aspiration which tends to be called into question. The temptation will be strong under these conditions to limit oneself to a positivism which will declare not merely insoluble, but even void of meaning these fundamental questions regarding the essence or the destiny of man to which science can provide no answer. This temptation can and must be surmounted by the very act of a freedom which acknowledges itself as irreducible to all the data of positive knowledge. But here arises a new temptation of idealistic pride, which sets up this freedom as an absolute, and leads if not to the express negation of being, at least to its endless paring down. It is up to freedom, come to the point where it accedes to the greatest self-awareness, to liberate itself in some way from itself, I mean by this, from its perverse disposition to affirm its own self-sufficiency. And this liberation is none other than the act of humility by which it immolates itself before grace.

One thus perceives how the calling into question or the interrogation of oneself changes at the extreme into a summons which is in fact the unique act of religious consciousness, and which can perhaps never be converted but ficticiously into an affirmation or a *statement*. This is what I have always called the invocation, that invocation which one could formulate like this: you who alone possess the secret of what I am and of what I am capable of becoming.

But perhaps this ultimate transmutation is itself, in the last analysis, but the work of grace, provided that he who has felt its mysterious work taking place in him accepts to open himself to it.

I cannot do better than to cite in conclusion these few lines borrowed from the admirable testimony of a young Jewish philosophy student, a convert to Catholicism, who died in the hell of Auschwitz: "I look at myself as I appear to myself. An unhealthy and chimerical child, burning for the good in intention, but without vigor if it is a question of struggling; the body weak, the intelligence (the intelligence of which I was so proud) greatly diminished. The temperament worn out. What can I do in reality? My professional value as a student of philosophy is very slight: I am far behind my comrades at once for knowledge, the urge to speak and to write, the authority necessary for leading a class . . . Well, this miserable being of mine will be justified, I have the feeling, if I offer it. It even is already, since there are those to whom I bring some comfort. But, O flesh, be not proud. I want to be but a servant."[1]

1. *Lettres de Jacques Lévy,* en dépôt aux editions André Borre, p. 152.

PART TWO

Human Uneasiness

CHAPTER I

Uneasiness, Anxiety, Anguish

Whoever seeks to find his bearings on the terrain which we are going to have to pass through in the course of these causeries devoted to *uneasiness* and *anxiety* is bound to proceed first of all to certain distinctions of terminology, if only to find very soon that they have but a rather relative value. If we refer to the *Littré,* we will note that it establishes the following gradation between uneasiness, anxiety, and anguish. "In uneasiness [*inquiétude*]," we are told, "it is the physical sensation which dominates almost exclusively, although in common parlance one sometimes uses the word in a moral or psychical sense. Yet one does not find in uneasiness the sensation of constriction, of something which oppresses. In anguish [*angoisse*], on the contrary, there would intervene a sensation of oppression of the epigastrium, accompanied by a great difficulty in breathing and by an excessive sadness. On the other hand, it is only in anxiety [*anxiété*] that one would find a state of trouble and agitation with a feeling of discomfort and oppression in the precordial region."

As I indicated, these distinctions cannot be taken word for word, and in particular the characterization of uneasiness is subject to caution. For my part, I would be inclined to dispute that the physical sensation is here dominant. On the other hand, there is controversy over the sense in which one should take, respectively, the terms of anxiety and anguish. At the end of the nineteenth century, Brissaud attempted to introduce here a quite precise distinction. According to him, anguish would be a physical phenomenon, anxiety on the contrary a purely psychical phenomenon; and if they are often concomitant, they could in certain cases occur separately. Anguish, he was to say at the Twelfth Congress of Alienist and Neurological Doctors, "is a physical disorder which is translated by a sensation of constriction, of smothering; anxiety is a psychical disorder which is translated by a feeling of indefinable insecurity." This distinction thus formulated was to be adopted by many French psychiatrists. But it has been in my opinion rightly contested in recent years, in particular by Mme. Juliette Boutonier in her book on *Angoisse*. What one can say is that the anxious person has much more violent reactions than the anguished person. He wrings his hands, abandons himself to despair, worries, whereas anguish is "the pain which cannot cry." The anxious person, more combative, struggles against the misfortune or the danger; the anguished person is overwhelmed by the emotion which paralyzes him. Anxiety is, as it were, envenomed by incertitude: when we know by a brief message that one of the persons who are closest to us is in danger of death, when we can find out nothing further and insurmountable obstacles prevent us from hurrying to his bedside, when we must wait for days on end to discover and implement a means of going to him, then it is anxiety which becomes our life. Let us evoke, for example, the atrocious personal situations which the line of demarcation multiplied under the Occupation.

But it is perfectly clear to my eyes that the anxiety thus described and illustrated can in no way be separated from uneasiness. In proportion as the latter becomes more precise and intensified, in proportion as the vise tightens, it tends to become anxiety.

We will see later on that in the perspective of existential philosophy on the one hand, and of psychoanalysis on the other, the term *anguish* has been taken in a more and more profound, a more and more fundamental acceptation. Let us say right away with Mme. Boutonier that in anguish it is not only the body, but above all the mind which seems more immobile than in anxiety. One thinks of nothing in particular, one lives anguish more than one thinks it, whereas one thinks anxiety as much as one lives it. The comparison between anguish and vertigo is very instructive here. If you consider the man seized by vertigo on the narrow cliff path where anguish has brought him to a halt, you do not see him fidget or even wring his hands. You do not imagine him for an instant explaining to you the nature of his vertigo. Whereas the anxious person seeks to get rid of his anxiety by doing something, were it by discussing with himself, the anguished person can no longer do anything but freeze in his anguish, he is somehow paralyzed. This last indication is very important. It has been remarked with reason, and we will have to remember it later, that in the case of vertigo as in anguish, there is in truth no alternative before which I find myself: I am at the same time the person to whom the alternative offers itself and the one who offers it. I am this very alternative, it only exists through me and in me. I am too closely one with anguish to have even the illusion of dominating it. I am thus this quartered unity, and it is because there is quartering that there is ambivalence.

But how can one help seeing that by emphasizing this charteristic we rejoin uneasiness, which also, at least when it reaches a certain depth, becomes quartering.

From this moment on, I am inclined personally to agree completely with the Spanish psychiatrist Lopez Ibor, when in his work on *La agonia del psicoanàlisis* he declared that for him anguish and uneasiness are one and the same phenomenon. We will simply have to recognize later that it is appropriate to distinguish diverse directions or orientations, so that uneasiness, for example, can be considered at times as paralyzing or even sterilizing, at times, on the contrary, as fecund and even somehow creative.

The strictly philosophical—and not exclusively psychological—interest attached to our problem is obviously linked to this ambiguity—one should perhaps say, to this ambivalence—which characterizes uneasiness. How can it be that according to the slant which we adopt to consider it, it can appear to us either as a shackle or as a stimulant? This double possibility can only have its principle in the metaphysical situation which is that of man. It is, moreover, inseparable—one must insist upon it—from an incertitude which bears upon values themselves and which finds an illustration in daily life, on the scale of collectivities and not of individuals alone. It is indeed clear that social or religious traditionalism will always be inclined to regard uneasiness with suspicion and will even sometimes go so far as to interpret it as the mark of the Luciferian spirit. But in a different perspective, one will be led to salute uneasiness as the condition of all progress, nay, of all genuine creation. There are grounds for asking oneself, in regard to the philosophers of existence and also in regard to Gide, the panegyrist of uneasiness, within what limits uneasiness can be justified or even encouraged, when beyond these limits it is in danger of degenerating into a destructive principle. One could not, of course, proceed to a determina-

70

tion of this kind without a great deal of prudence and flexibility. As almost always when it is a question of spiritual things, one can at bottom only limit oneself to specifying directions, far from formulating dogmatic statements which would run a great risk of deforming the subtle realities which one intends to treat.

We must yet observe that this perspective, as wide as it is, is far from being the only one, and that from the point of view of spirituality—or if you wish, of the relation between the believing soul and God—, there will be reason to ask oneself what room should be made for uneasiness. Is not uneasiness incompatible with the unshakable confidence of him who rests without fear, without ulterior motive, upon the absolute goodness of the Creator? I will not treat quietism directly, but it is clear that it precisely corresponded to this concern to banish everything which could come to trouble the believing soul. Quietism as such has disappeared, or if it has survived, it is only as a living disposition in certain souls, without any longer materializing doctrinally. But here again a permanent problem subsists: that of knowing what sort of uneasiness is not only compatible with genuine faith, but also, strictly speaking, required in order for faith not to degenerate into an almost passive abandon in which the soul, far from being able to develop or actualize its most precious virtualities, is in danger of growing numb.

My general plan is thus not to limit myself to passing in review the attitudes which have been adopted in the face of this problem by a certain number of great minds: my ambition would be, by means of this examination, to manage to take a stand, so far as it is possible, in the face of contemporary uneasiness. For one can doubt that at any other period of the past the trouble was more universal and more profound.

71

CHAPTER II

The Uneasy Person as Self-Tormentor

THERE is, as you know, a comedy of Terence entitled *The Self-Tormentor*. Now, one could say that these words furnish us one of the best possible characterizations of the uneasy person. We constantly use in day-to-day life the verb "to worry oneself" without paying sufficient attention to what is implied by the reflexive form; for "to worry oneself" is really to be one's own torturer. In fact, nothing is more important than to interrogate oneself regarding this paradox, that is, to ask oneself how it can be that in certain cases—and in the most active way—we should become our own enemy. This possibility can only be deeply rooted in our structure.

The affinity has sometimes been stressed between uneasiness and doubt. But it is quite necessary to see that doubt taken in itself is in no way uneasiness. It can even have a euphoric character in the skeptic who settles down comfortably in his skepticism. Doubt truly coincides with uneasiness only when it becomes anguishing, let us even say tormenting, that is, for a person who feels literally imprisoned, but who makes repeated efforts to get out, each one of these attempts contributing in fact, however, to rivet his chains more tightly.

It is clear that such a disposition is linked to what contemporary psychology calls introversion, that is, to a person's being turned towards himself and not towards exterior reality. One can say theoretically—I introduce this reservation because in such a domain there is always room for exceptions or anomalies—one can say that a person energetically engaged in action is nearly immunized against uneasiness such as I have just defined it, and that, inversely, inaction tends to favor it. It is for this same reason that insomnia so often helps to develop what one calls the blues. Everything is really as if anguishing thoughts profited in order to impose themselves upon us from the fact that our inaction leaves them a clear field. This is only a somewhat mythological way of expressing oneself, for these anguishing thoughts do not, after all, possess an existence independent of us. They are somehow ourselves, but an "ourselves" ordinarily inhibited by the necessities of life. Life normally implies, indeed, a whole set of summonses or solicitations to which we have to respond in the most precise way. One should distinguish, moreover, between the cases in which these responses occur automatically—and those in which we have to bring into play a power of initiative or invention. One can affirm that the more this power exerts itself, the less we are in danger of letting ourselves be alienated by uneasiness. I purposely use this verb "alienate," which one rarely uses in this context. But it must be taken in its rigorous etymological acceptation. To alienate is to estrange. Now, the uneasy person tends indeed to be estranged even from those closest to him; between them and him there opens up a more and more impassable gap. And naturally we discern here the absolutely imperceptible passage from the cases called normal to the cases called pathological. The uneasy person, as such, almost inevitably becomes distrustful. To be sure, he distrusts first of all himself, but this distrust of oneself cannot help in the long run but bring about distrust towards others. This is particularly clear in the case of the man who considers himself unworthy of being loved. How could he not come to consider suspect everything which presents itself to him as the testimony of sentiments which he does not believe he can inspire.

It would be interesting to ask oneself in this perspective whether distrust towards others is not usually linked to a certain lack of inward assurance, without, of course, this lack necessarily becoming self-conscious. One would have to allow for a great deal of nuance; one ought in particular to take care not to confuse lack of assurance with modesty or humility. It is probable that most of the time this lack can be interpreted as a sort of mental crack due to a trauma usually taken place in childhood. In this regard, we will never be prudent enough, vigilant enough, when in the presence of a child we let ourselves be led to judge him. For many, uneasiness probably stems from an earlier mortification. It is, of course, obvious that this mortification was not necessarily apparent, above all in a proud child who was all the more careful to hide his wound as it was more bitter. It is also very possible that this child was not, strictly speaking, conscious of the humiliation inflicted upon him. But I will note here—and this remark has an extremely general psychological import—that the term *consciousness* is dangerously ambiguous, and this ambiguity affects in the most unfortunate way the use of the words *subconscious* and *unconscious*. If I say that this humiliation—or in psychoanalytic terms, this trauma— was not necessarily conscious, I mean that the child can very well not have said to himself: I am humiliated. Everything can very well have happened below—let us not say all consciousness, but reflective or simply articulate consciousness.

I have considered here, of course, only one aspect, though a very important one, of the psychology of the uneasy person. The simplest reflection shows that uneasiness is capable of radiating in the most diverse directions. The jealous person, for example, can be considered an uneasy person; and in certain cases the same is true of the miser, although one cannot say that avarice in itself is based on uneasiness. But I am here thinking very particularly of that avarice which is connected with the fear of lacking the necessities of life. Such examples help to bring out the role almost invariably played in uneasiness by a certain proliferation which is imaginative but which always develops in the same direction. I think that one could without exaggeration compare this unhealthy proliferation to the anormal histological development observed in certain diseases, particularly in cancerous diseases. One sees here how the uneasy person can so often be obsessed, and naturally again this time we distinctly perceive the passage from the normal to the pathological. I will also note in passing that we are here in the presence of a certain paradox. For one could be tempted at first to suppose that uneasiness is above all a lack of stability. But how could an unstable person become obsessed? One must no doubt answer that here as always the psychological reality is far more complex and elusive than one is tempted to believe at first glance. For there can be unstable persons who are not uneasy, instability being then linked to a certain levity, that which one finds in very superficial people. If the uneasy person can be called unstable, it is in a very particular sense and insofar as he is in search of an equilibrium which he nonetheless feels repugnance for. We thus find once again at the end of this analysis the inner contradiction which somehow undermines the very existence of the uneasy person.

It is therefore fitting to make it a matter of principle that there is not and cannot be an absolutely clear-cut difference between the uneasy and the anxious person. It would not be in conformity to the general plan which I am following here to expatiate upon psychopathology strictly speaking. Nonetheless, it would be useful very rapidly to recall here what conception a master of psychopathology such as Pierre Janet has developed of anguish. Faithful to the objective method which is his, he makes a point of always considering feelings themselves as conductors. "Anguish," he says, "always accompanies a reaction of failure in regard to any act, and it is more or less great according to the importance of the act arrested by the reaction of failure. We have waged a great battle in order to defend the soil of the fatherland, the battle is lost. The sentiment which the soldier feels, which every man of the country feels, is a great anguish. We have prepared an examination, we have written the compositions, we learn that we have failed: this is anguish. We struggle at the bedside of a sick child, we have tried everything and death is approaching: we are anguished." But one can think with Mme. Boutonier that the language here is lacking in rigor and that, for example, the examinee who has failed feels not anguish, but sadness, humiliation, etc. Anguish rather seems only to arise here before the failure, when the failure seems to loom up as a menace. If we appeal to our memories of examinations, we will recall, I believe, having experienced a feeling of genuine anguish when, in the course of an examination involving a translation or a problem to solve, we discovered that the time was passing, that the moment when we would have to hand in our paper was approaching, without our having yet successfully finished the problem or translation. What is altogether characteristic here is the role which the temporal shrinking which one feels plays in the creation of the feeling of anguish, with the imminence of a dreaded expiration. I believe I should draw attention particularly to this point. For nowhere, in my opinion, does anguish appear more clearly in its specificity. But we also see that anguish is no longer, strictly speaking, uneasiness, or if you wish, that it is like an ultimate state which uneasiness tends towards when it passes from the diffuse state to what one could call the concentrated state.

I will leave aside here the strictly psychoanalytical interpretation and above all the infinitely debatable idea that anguish begins in the individual with the trauma of birth, this trauma corresponding to the rupture of the biological situation of equilibrium in which the foetus found itself. As ingenious as it may be, this idea has an almost mythological character, it is beyond all possible verification. As far as I am concerned, I do not think we have to take it into account when we seek to understand wherein uneasiness or anguish consist.

CHAPTER III

Uneasiness Condemned by the Sages

I HAVE attempted to show, first of all, that the uneasy person can be defined as a "self-tormentor," and it is evident enough that if uneasiness is considered in this perspective, it can hardly not appear as an evil. One could thus not be surprised that the sages are in agreement in condemning it. One could even go so far as to say that the principal objective of wisdom such as it has been defined at all times consists after all in exorcising uneasiness. This is immediately comprehensible, since the sage is preoccupied with realizing for himself a spiritual equilibrium as stable as possible, and secondarily, with putting his disciples in a position to attain to it for themselves. The term *ataraxia,* which is of Greek origin, designates precisely this absence of trouble, of inner agitation, which Epicurus, for example, considered as the ideal towards which every reasonable person should tend. In this perspective, as also in that of the Stoics of whom I will speak in a moment, uneasiness is invariably linked to a passional state from which the sage intends to cure us. It is, in fact, knowledge which will have the fortunate effect of delivering us from illusory beliefs which throw disorder into our soul. This could be illustrated in many ways. I will choose the passage of *De Natura Rerum* where Lucretius, a faithful disciple of Epicurus, undertakes to demonstrate on the one hand that the soul is mortal and that consequently the idea of sanctions, of superterrestrial punishments is chimerical, and on the other that, death being a pure and simple annihilation, we will not have to suffer in any way from being deprived of goods which appear so precious to us today and which we cannot resign ourselves to lose.

"When you see a man lament over himself," says Lucretius, "at the thought that after death, once his body is abandoned, he will decay, or will be devoured by flames or by the jaws of wild beasts, you can say that his voice rings false, and that some secret thorn is hidden in his heart despite his affected refusal to believe that any sentiment could subsist in him in death. In my opinion, he does not harmonize what he declares, he does not give his true reasons: he does not radically tear himself away and take refuge from life, but rather even unbeknown to him he supposes that something in him survives. Indeed, the living person who imagines that his body, after death, will be torn apart by birds and beasts of prey pities his own person: he does not separate himself from this object, he does not distinguish himself enough from this outstretched corpse, he confuses himself with it, and standing at its side he lends it his sensibility. This is why he is indignant at having been created mortal, without seeing that in actual death there will be no other himself who, still alive, could deplore his own loss, and remain on his feet, groaning to see himself lying on the ground, the prey of beasts or flames." One sees clearly here that uneasiness partakes of dread, that in the eyes of the sage it appears imputable to a sophism of the imagination which it is up to rational thought to bring to light. The sage esteems—rightly or wrongly—that this refutation, if it is understood, should put an end to the uneasiness, that is, to the painful agitation to which we are prey before wisdom has delivered us from it.

Among the Stoics, particularly in Epicurus, it is the distinction between what depends on us and what does not depend on us which will be utilized so as to free us from uneasiness. The postulate of Stoic morality will consist all told in making it a matter of principle that if I want to behave not as an animal or as a child, but as an adult and reasonable person, I must train myself to be indifferent to what it is not in my power to change. One could say that I thus realize a genuine economy of strength, since I cease fruitlessly wearing myself out in recriminations against destiny or, what is even more disastrous, in vain attempts to transform in the direction of my desires what in reality depends on an immutable order on which I have no hold.

Marcus Aurelius revives—on his own account, of course—the distinction between the things which depend on us and those which do not depend on us. "All that I am amounts to this: the flesh, the breath, the inner guide. Give up books, no longer let yourself be distracted, it is no longer allowed you; but at the thought that you are at death's door, despise the flesh: it is mere mud and blood, bones and a fine network of nerves, veins and arteries. And see, too, what your breath is: wind, and not always the same, for at each moment you expel it in order to breathe in another again. There thus remains in the third place the inner guide. Do you think of it? Permit it no longer to remain a slave, to obey egotistical instincts like a marionette, to get angry with present destiny, nor to apprehend that to come."

I admit that I do not agree with M. Aimé Puech when in his preface to the French edition of the *Meditations* he accuses Marcus Aurelius of being only a good pupil of the Stoics, one of those pupils who are overly docile and who exaggerate. What seems to me to confer a value upon the *Meditations* is that we feel the author perpetually in dialogue with himself, and we are permitted to conjecture what in him would like to resist the exhortations which he addresses to himself. "Will you ever be, O my soul, good, upright, one, bare, more manifest than the body which envelops you? Will you ever relish the disposition to find everything good and to love everything? Will you ever be satisfied, without need, without regret, without desire for anything at all, animate or inanimate, which gives you pleasure, nor for a respite in order to enjoy pleasure longer, nor for another place, another region, a happier climate, a more harmonious society . . . Will you ever be such that you could live in the common city of gods and men without raising the least complaint against them nor incurring their blame?" How could one help but recognize the moving quality of this interrogation. "The soul of man," he says further, "dishonors itself above all when, insofar as it depends on it, it becomes an abscess and as it were an excrescence of the world." Against this dishonor, against this degradation, a single and unique recourse: wisdom, philosophy which merges with wisdom. "It consists in keeping watch over the inner god, in order that he remain exempt of affront and injury, triumph over pleasures and pains, do nothing rashly, abstain from lies and dissimulation, have no need for others to do or not do this or that; moreover, that he accept what happens and constitutes his lot as coming from that origin, whatever it be, from which he himself came; and above all that he await death in favorable dispositions, seeing in it nothing but the dissolution of the elements of which each living being is formed."

But one could not insist too much upon the fact that an ethic of this kind is based on the idea of an harmonious cosmos, the whole being necessarily good. "The universal substance is docile and plastic. The reason which governs has in itself no motive for doing evil, for it has no maliciousness, it does no evil to anything, and nothing receives any harm from it. Now, everything begins and ends according to its designs."

But there is perhaps reason to remark that in such a metaphysical context there is hardly room for anguish such as it has appeared to us in the course of our first study.

Let us observe once and for all that in such a perspective the domain of uneasiness appears as co-extensive with the domain of desire and fear. It is no less evident, moreover, that the imagination, insofar as it puts itself in the service of desire and fear, appears as impure, precisely on account of the complicities to which it so easily lends itself. One can thus say that a rationalist philosophy centered on the idea of an eternal order, or else of a necessity immanent in the universe, cannot help but adopt, in regard to uneasiness, a position on the whole identical to that which I have defined above. The attitude of a Spinoza can in this sense be regarded as exemplary, for no one has pushed the affirmation of this order and of this necessity to its extreme consequences more than he. The fourth book of the *Ethics,* following the third which deals with the affections—or in contemporary language, the passions—, treats human servitude. Now what is this servitude if not that to which we succumb when we let ourselves be led astray by the imagination? But here again, from the moment we rise to genuine knowledge, we deliver ourselves from all this inner confusion to which we are prey if we fall into the snares of the imagination.

It is naturally impossible to enter here into the detail of the system, certainly one of the most coherent which the history of philosophy presents to us. What is important is simply to recognize that in such a doctrine, uneasiness appears as the inner fatality to which anyone finds himself subject who has not proceeded to a rational rectification or purification which alone can permit him to attain to genuine freedom. The last book of the *Ethics* is in fact entitled "Of Human Freedom." But this freedom is defined at once by the knowledge and even the love of the absolute necessity which merges with the being in the unfolding of its modes.

We will soon have to see how, in a different metaphysical and religious perspective, uneasiness can take on a positive value, far from being reduced to a state of agitation from which we would have to cure ourselves as from a bad fever.

CHAPTER IV

Uneasiness in the Perspective of the Gospel

WE have seen that, in a philosophy like that of Spinoza, or for all thought which claims affinity with the Stoic postulate, or perhaps with a naturalism of some kind, uneasiness can be considered only as an evil. But one must recognize, on the other hand, that in these same perspectives this evil appears as essentially curable: the philosopher undertakes to inculcate in us a certain method which permits whoever practices it in its rigor to arrive at a certain serenity which the vicissitudes of existence could not get the better of. But it is evident that the horizon is transformed if man is considered as being the free creature of a transcendent god and if his destination is salvation, that is, a certain harmony to be established or restored between him and the superior power which has called him into being; or if this creature is called upon to acknowledge or admit that he is in a fallen state resulting from sin. If the metaphysical situation of the human being is thus defined, it clearly appears that, in a certain way, he is doomed to uneasiness. I say: in a certain way; I mean by that that it is not only normal, but necessary and even highly desirable that he experience at the outset a profound trouble linked to the metaphysical fact that on account of sin he is not as he should be. But moreover, he could not think of counting on his own strength alone to bring about this transformation, at the term of which he would recuperate the blessings which he has lost. In order for this transformation to be possible, he will be obliged to lend himself to the transcendent action of grace; and it is to the degree in which he lends himself to it, but in which he also has the redoubtable possibility of refusing it, that he behaves as a free being. Yet, from the moment that the creature finds himself placed under the obligation of seeing in himself this mysterious articulation of freedom and grace, it is impossible that he not experience a certain uneasiness—an uneasiness linked to the sentiment of his fundamental unworthiness. One can even go further and say that if this uneasiness were foreign to him, it would be the proof that he were settled down in a certain self-complacency which excludes all genuine spiritual progress.

Under these conditions, we see ourselves forced to observe that for a Christian consciousness, the value judgment made on uneasiness can by no means be the same as for a Stoic or a Spinozist. To be sure, as I have already had occasion to remark, we are here in a domain in which it is difficult to take one's bearings, in which the passage from the normal to the pathological takes place imperceptibly. Let us observe, moreover, that the word *normal* in this perspective no longer fits the situation of man, for he bears within him, as it were, a lesion imputable to sin. One can even go so far as to maintain that this lesion is all the more profound as it is less recognized by the one affected by it.

Yet this does not mean, of course, that Christianity implies the justification or the validation of all forms of uneasiness whatever. We have seen that at the limit, uneasiness can be regarded as co-extensive with the domain of fear and desire. It would be contrary to all truth to claim that Christianity implies anything resembling an absolution of human passions. This would be an absurd and strictly scandalous alteration of a profound truth which I would tend to formulate as follows: the Christian cannot fail to take pity on even the worst deviations of his brothers, far from looking down on them with condescension or scorn, as the sage tends to do who believes himself exempt or cured of these weaknesses. But above all and in a complementary way the Christian, because he knows himself to be a sinner, discovers in himself the analogue of these weaknesses and does not claim any qualification for judging them. And if he were to judge them, he would himself become guilty of the Pharisaism so expressly condemned in the Gospels.

To avoid a misunderstanding which could only favor the most ruinous misconceptions, it would therefore be fitting to distinguish, within uneasiness, on the one hand the disorders of all kinds to which the sinful soul is exposed, and on the other the discomfort, perhaps at first secret and inarticulate, to which it is prey by the fact of its fundamental situation, but also the aspiration—it too no doubt vague at the outset—which bears it to the encounter with grace, without which salvation would remain a mere wish devoid of all efficacy.

It would be quite easy to show that the object of the Gospel parables is in many cases to undermine in us a rationalism whose inevitable result would be to reinforce in us the tendency to be complacent with ourselves in the consideration of our merits. Let us reread, for example, the text of St. Luke: "Two men went up into the temple to pray, one a Pharisee and the other a tax collector. The Pharisee stood and prayed thus with himself, 'God, I thank thee that I am not like other men, extortioners, unjust, adulterers, or even like this tax collector. I fast twice a week, I give tithes of all that I get.' But the tax collector, standing far off, would not even lift up his eyes to heaven, but beat his breast, saying, 'God, be merciful to me a sinner!' I tell you, this man went down to his house justified rather than the other; for every one who exalts himself will be humbled, but he who humbles himself will be exalted" (Lk. 18, 10–14).

The end of the parable of the prodigal son is no less significant. When the elder son, coming in from the fields and hearing music and dancing, asked a servant what it meant, he was told: "Your brother has come, and your father has killed the fatted calf, because he has received him safe and sound." But he became angry and refused to go in. His father came out to entreat him, but he answered his father: " 'Lo, these many years I have served you, and I have never disobeyed your command; yet you never gave me a kid, that I might make merry with my friends. But when this son of yours came, who has devoured your living with harlots, you killed for him the fatted calf!' And he said to him, 'Son, you are always with me, and all that is mine is yours. It was fitting to make merry and be glad, for this your brother was dead, and is alive; he was lost, and is found" (Lk. 15, 27–32).

One could easily multiply the examples. Let us now put ourselves into the consciousness of one who has heard these parables. Would he not be incited to free himself from the self-satisfaction which one is inclined to who feels himself on good terms with a certain established order? And this lack of self-satisfaction is none other than uneasiness. We see here distinctly how it can be fruitful, how it can become the active principle of a spiritual dynamism oriented towards transcendence.

Yet this aspect, essential as it may be, could not be separated without abuse from a different though on the whole complementary aspect. In Luke we read: "Do not be anxious about your life, what you shall eat, nor about your body, what you shall put on. For life is more than food, and the body more than clothing . . . Consider the lilies, how they grow; they neither toil nor spin; yet I tell you, even Solomon in all his glory was not arrayed like one of these. But if God so clothes the grass which is alive in the field today and tomorrow is thrown into the oven, how much more will he clothe you, O men of little faith! And do not seek what you are to eat and what you are to drink, nor be of anxious mind. For all the nations of the world seek these things; and your father knows that you need them. Instead, seek his kingdom, and these things shall be yours as well" (Lk. 12, 22-31).

If one looks closely, what is here not only advised against but forbidden is worry rather than uneasiness. But we know well that in daily life worry and uneasiness are hardly separable. A text like that which I have quoted could appear to recommend a sort of quietism; but this would not be a legitimate interpretation. At bottom, what is here affirmed to us is that we have to worry not about the material conditions of our existence, but exclusively about doing the will of our heavenly Father. From the moment we behave as faithful servants, we can be assured, we are told, that we will not lack what is precisely indispensable to us in order to accomplish our task. Would one be mistaken in suggesting that what is implied here is the notion of a certain pact between the Creator and the creature? It would be impious to suppose that where the creature proves faithful, God could for His part not respond to the confidence which His servant places in Him. I do not press this point, and I will be the first to admit that Gospel texts can rarely be interpreted in a contractual sense. It is clear that by His grace God always exceeds what we could reasonably expect from Him, since we can assign no limit to His mercy. On the other hand, would it not be a sacrilege to admit that His justice could be at fault? And this would be precisely the case if he who has placed his hope in Him should find himself abandoned. Let us acknowledge that this is an idea which should not be made too explicit, but rather remain as it were suspended in the spiritual atmosphere in which the destiny of the Children of Light unfolds throughout Christian history.

What remains indisputable in any case is that in the perspective of the Gospel there is one sense and one only in which uneasiness finds its justification, on the condition, of course, that it not degenerate into morbid scruples and obsessions. There exists a psychopathology of religious consciousness which, precisely, denounces these sicknesses. But it would be contrary to all truth not to differentiate here between uneasiness strictly speaking, insofar as it is grounded in the very being of the creature, and its deformed or aberrant expressions.

CHAPTER V

Uneasiness in St. Augustine

WE have been able to realize that in a Christian perspective it is not only possible, but no doubt indispensable, to find an internal justification for uneasiness considered as the movement by which the human soul, denouncing all complacency in itself and in the sensible world as well, shakes itself free from itself and comes forward somehow to meet grace. It is in this sense that one must understand the famous phrase of the invocation which opens the *Confessions* of St. Augustine. "You are great, Lord, and infinitely worthy of praise; great is your power and incalculable your wisdom, and it is you whom man, a puny part of your creation, wants to praise, man who bears with him everywhere his mortality, who bears with him the testimony of his sin, and the proof that you resist the arrogant. And yet he wants to praise you, this man, a puny part of your creation. It is you who urge him to seek his joy in your praise, for you have made us for yourself, and our heart is uneasy until it rests in you."

But immediately afterwards, St. Augustine interrogates himself regarding the meaning and even the possibility of such an invocation. "Is there in me," he asks, "a place where my God could come?" "Since I myself exist, why do I ask you to come into me who would not exist if you were not in me? . . ." "I would thus not exist, O my God, I would absolutely not exist if you were not in me. Or rather, I would not exist if I were not in you, from whom, through whom, and in whom all things exist." And immediately the questions multiply which are born from the apparent contradiction between divine ubiquity and the fact that I seem to ask God to come into me, as if He were not already in me.

We are thus certainly in the presence here of an interrogation which deserves the name of metaphysical or religious uneasiness, for it is by no means a question of a mere speculative curiosity. The question asked matters in the most essential, the most intimate way to the very life of my soul.

In fact, as Etienne Gilson says in his *The Christian Philosophy of St. Augustine,* the foundation of this uneasiness resides in the radical insufficiency, in the essential want from which man suffers as a creature drawn from nothingness. "Not being self-sufficient in the order of being, he could be self-sufficient neither in the order of knowledge nor in the order of action: but this very want from which he suffers orients him towards Him who alone can satisfy him. Whence the fruitful uneasiness which unceasingly troubles man but which saves him in that, made for God, it permits him to find in God alone peace and repose." St. Augustine will observe in *The City of God* that if our nature were our own work, we would have been able to engender our own wisdom: "Our love originating with ourselves and tendered back to ourselves would suffice to assure us beatitude, and we would not have need of a good foreign to ourselves to enjoy it: but since our nature has God as the author of its being, it is beyond doubt that in order to be initiated into truth [*ut vera sapiamus*], we need to be instructed by him." It is to Him that it belongs to dispense to us what St. Augustine calls *Suavitas intima,* which I would tend to translate by the words: "the intimate or inner balm" which is the principle of our beatitude.

It is of the greatest importance, I believe, to observe in this context that the so evident originality of Augustinian thought is linked in part to the fact that St. Augustine was a convert, and that he was thus led, by reflecting upon his conversion, to an extraordinarily precise awareness of grace, of the work of grace in us. The *Confessions* constitute a testimony of a certainly unsurpassed value on this capital fact of conversion which, in a rationalist perspective, will always remain unintelligible, and which therefore those who approach it from the outside will be fatally inclined to deform or even to reject. There is not and there cannot be any common measure between the living experience of the convert and the way in which one attempts to account for it who, not participating in this experience, tends to substitute something else for it. I believe I am not mistaken in saying that the reflection upon this inevitable disparity constitutes one of the points of departure of the philosophy of existence such as it has developed among the moderns. In this sense one has seen in St. Augustine, not without reason, a precursor of what one has called by a barbarous name which I for my part reject: existentialism.

Do these remarks divert us from our subject? Obviously not. For we must always recall that uneasiness takes on a positive value in the regard of a consciousness which has recognized in itself the operation of grace, and this must, of course, be repeated in regard to Pascal.

Let us note right now, however, that the reverse is not true, or at least does not seem true, and that there can be cases in which uneasiness is *valorized* without him who feels and acknowledges its benefits appearing to himself in any way visited by grace. But in St. Augustine and in all those who are of his descent, this connection is evident.

It must be added that the relationship to the Gospel themes that I previously mentioned is immediate. In the eighth book of the *Confessions,* for example, St. Augustine expresses himself as follows:

"Good Lord, what happens in man, that he rejoice more over the salvation of a soul when he despaired of it and when it has been delivered from a graver peril than when he had always preserved some hope regarding it, or when the peril had been less serious? . . . What happens in the soul, that it feel more joy in finding or recovering what it loves than in keeping it constantly? Many other examples attest to it; everything is full of evidence which cries to us: it is so! . . . A loved one is sick; his pulse reveals that he is in danger; all those who desire his recovery are sick in their soul at the same time as he. Improvement sets in. He walks about without yet having recuperated his former strength, and already there is a gladness such as there never was when he previously went about in full strength and health.

"What does this mean, O Lord my God? . . . Ah yes, how sublime you are in the heights and profound in the abysses! You never withdraw from us, and yet how hard it is to reach you!"

One recognizes here the eminent value of this uneasiness which moves the human soul to pass ceaselessly from object to object (I again cite Etienne Gilson), as if the full satisfaction which one attainment has not given it could be given it by another, whereas in reality, as long as this quest lasts, even supposing that it lead us but from truth to truth, there is no peace for thought, and consequently no beatitude. But what is beatitude, then, if not the presence to the soul of an ultimate truth which is at the same time the unique Good, since it is God. But this Good which we covet, this truth to which we aspire, is already somehow in us, and it is through recourse to reflection on memory that St. Augustine undertakes to make us catch a glimpse of what may be the nature of this immanence of God in him who seeks Him. One must here refer to the unforgettable pages of the tenth book of the *Confessions* in which St. Augustine, in the presence of the mystery of memory, is struck with an absolutely religious wonder. "Even when my tongue falls silent, when my throat remains without a sound, I sing as much as I can, and the images of colors may well be there, but they do not intervene or interrupt while I ply the other treasure which I owe to my ears. Thus I run through at my pleasure the impressions which the other senses have furnished and accumulated in me . . . All this goes on, in the interior of myself, in the ample palace of the memory . . . Great, O my God, is this power of memory; O yes, quite great. It is an immense, an infinite sanctuary; who has ever penetrated to its depth! Yet it is but a power of my mind, linked to my nature: but I cannot conceive completely what I am. The mind is thus too narrow to contain itself! Then where does what it cannot contain of itself flow back? Would it be outside of it and not in it? But how does it not contain it? This thought dumbfounds me with astonishment, and I feel stricken with stupefaction."

I am thus, as it were, essentially unequal to myself, I am too great for myself. By fathoming this mystery, St. Augustine will be led to recognize first of all that God Himself is in some way in our memory, but that this would naturally be inconceivable if the memory were in us a sort of container. Memory must be in us more than ourselves, so that finally it is in God that we find God. In *De Trinitate* St. Augustine will thus be led to say that when the soul remembers its Lord because it has received the Spirit, it is well aware that it is instructed by the inner agency which the Spirit exerts upon it. It is because God is everywhere in totality that the soul lives and moves in Him and that it can remember Him.

We would thus not love God if He did not love us first of all Himself. There is no doctrine which is more absolutely dominated by the idea that God is Love, and it has been rightly said that a doctrine is Augustinian to the extent that it tends more completely to organize itself around Charity.

It is thus quite clear that uneasiness is here but a ferment, or if you wish, a leaven, without which the soul could not, strictly speaking, be converted, since this leaven is also the work which God, which grace, performs in the depths of the creature.

CHAPTER VI

Uneasiness in Pascal

THERE would certainly be grounds, if one had the leisure, and as a prolongation of what I have said regarding St. Augustine, for showing by numerous examples how an entire form of Christian spirituality, and certainly not the least lofty, cannot be separated from a certain uneasiness which, far from presenting any pathological or morbid character, translates the situation of the believing soul in the presence of the transcendent God to whom it aspires to unite itself. I will cite but one text borrowed from the meditative prayers of William of St. Thierry, one of the greatest spiritual minds of the twelfth century.

"The apprehensive and bewildered soul prepares to pray to its God, always holding itself in its hands, as if to offer itself to you; it is afraid before what it knows, it is bewildered before what is new; in order to find you it is marked by the sign of the faith, but this sign cannot yet be of use to it; seeking your face, your face, Lord, it is in ignorance, in total non-recognition of what it seeks. The phantoms of its heart are an abomination to you like idols. The soul loves you, such as it knows you by faith, but the mind cannot see you. Burning with desire to see your face, to which it offers the sacrifice of its piety and its justice, its offerings and its holocausts, it becomes more flustered because it longs to see your face. And since it does not yet receive the illumination of your faith, whereas it believed itself in possession of this faith, it is sometimes bewildered to the point of almost thinking that it does not believe in you, and to the point of hating itself because it seems to it that it does not love you. It does not have to fear in you, this soul is anguished by the desire which it has of you, anguished not to love you, this soul which desires you to the point of scorning everything which exists, of scorning itself! How long, Lord, how long?"

One could say that uneasiness is not only inevitable but that it is absolutely salutary, in that is corresponds to the impatience of the believing soul which, because it still lives in the obscurity of faith, suffers from still being deprived of the Vision.

It is essential to remark that such an uneasiness is not, strictly speaking, anguish.

At the same period, St. Bernard's *Treatise on the Love of God* expresses with a singular force analogous conceptions which are very directly linked to Augustinianism. He denounces the circle in which the impious walk, who by a natural tendency desire to satisfy their appetite, and like madmen neglect what could bring them nearer to their end—not the end which consumes but which consummates. "The will, perverted in its exercise by sin, hurries towards what can satisfy it, vanity fools itself, iniquity lies to itself. But God is there who seeks us, who precedes us." St. Bernard undertakes to show us how, by what progressive steps, oriented by this God who is Love, the human soul will rise from the inferior stage where it can only love itself for itself to that where it no longer loves itself but for God and will finally attain to the perfection of love which is the portion of the blessed after the resurrection.

Here as in St. Augustine, uneasiness, it must be repeated, has by no means the character of anguish.

In Pascal, on the contrary, the difference between uneasiness and anguish often tends to disappear, and this even if one refuses to overemphasize, as certain moderns have done, what one could call the pre-romantic character of the Pascalian experience.

In reality, it is impossible for anyone who reflects upon uneasiness not to place Pascal in the center of his reflection. One can in fact affirm, I believe, that no one before the contemporaries (among whom I would readily place Kierkegaard, whose importance has only been recognized in our time), I say *no one,* has better known how to elucidate the roots of uneasiness considered as an essential or primary modality of human experience.

In this respect, it is appropriate to take the greatest account of the *Discours sur les Passions de l'Amour,*[1] which seems to date from Pascal's mundane period (1652–1653). I recall its opening lines here:

"Man is born to think, and he is not a moment without doing so; but the pure thoughts which would make him happy if he could always maintain them, fatigue and depress him. That is an uneventful life which he cannot accommodate himself to; he needs commotion and action, that is to say, it is necessary for him to be sometimes agitated by the passions of which he feels such lively and such deep sources in his heart." Pascal will then tell us that the passions which are the most suitable to man and which contain many others, are love and ambition. But how could one not see that the latter are in fact presented as modalities of uneasiness in the strongest sense of this word? At bottom, Pascal introduces us into the *cor irrequietum,* the "heart without repose," of which St. Augustine spoke. But one must immediately

1. The attribution of the *Discours* to Pascal is sometimes contested.

add that this heart is not separated from the thought which genuinely constitutes man as such. In the *Pensées* Pascal will say: "Our nature is in movement, complete repose is death." But let us not fail to remark that Pascal here follows Montaigne and that the "Apologie de Raymond Sebond" presents a wholly similar picture of natural man. "Man does not love to remain with himself," Pascal says further. "Yet he loves: he must thus seek elsewhere something to love. He can find it only in beauty, but since he is himself the most beautiful creature that God has ever formed, he must find in himself the model of that beauty which he seeks without." But this is more significant still: "The attachment to one and the same thought fatigues and ruins the mind of man. That is why for the solidity and duration of the pleasure of love one must sometimes not know that one loves; and this is not to commit an infidelity, for one does not love another; it is to recover strength in order to love better. This happens without one's thinking of it; the mind proceeds to it by itself, nature wants it; it demands it. But one must admit that it is a miserable result of human nature, and that one would be happier if one were not obliged to change thoughts; but there is no remedy."

This remarkable text, which anticipates in a surprising way the Proustian psychology of the intermittences of the heart, perfectly illustrates what one can regard, it seems to me, as the original conception of uneasiness in Pascal. As I indicted, what is here laid bare is the foundation of uneasiness, its roots in the very nature of man. When later, in the *Pensées,* he speaks of boredom, he will express himself in the same way: "Nothing is so unbearable to man as to be in full repose, without passions, without affairs, without amusements, without exertion. He then feels his nothingness, his abandonment, his insufficiency, his dependence, his impotence, his emptiness." It is this last word, this word *emptiness,* which should above all retain our attention here, for it permits us, it seems to me, to recognize the increase in depth which has been realized in the soul and mind of Pascal since the *Discours.* When we are at rest, we find ourselves almost inevitably put in the presence of our own inner emptiness, and this very emptiness is in reality intolerable to us. But there is more, there is the fact that through this emptiness we inevitably become aware of the misery of our condition, a "condition so miserable," says Pascal, "that nothing can console us when we think about it carefully." Whence the necessity of diversion: "The men who naturally sense their condition avoid nothing so much as repose, there is nothing they would not do to seek turmoil . . . They have a secret instinct which leads them to seek amusement and occupation abroad, and which comes from the sense of their continual miseries." But here Pascal will add another complementary remark, that the men have another secret instinct, which remains from the greatness of our first nature and makes them know that happiness is in fact found only in rest, and not in tumult. And from these two contrary instincts there forms in them an obscure project which hides from their view in the depths of their soul, exciting them to aim at rest through agitation, and always to imagine that the satisfaction which they do not have will come to them, if, by surmounting whatever difficulties they envisage, they can thereby open the door to rest.

But the diagnosis thus brought to bear upon the profound nature of human uneasiness amounts to recognizing that, in its depths, uneasiness is anguish, and Pascal thereby indisputably appears as the genuine precursor of the philosophies of existence to the extent that they see in anguish a privileged metaphysical category.

CHAPTER VII

From Pascal to Kierkegaard

WE have seen that the function of diversion according to Pascal consists in interposing a screen between us and the unbearable spectacle of our condition. In this sense one can say that diversion is itself the fruit of uneasiness. Let us be careful to note that this condition which is ours can be considered at the level of temporary moods or dispositions, but that a more profound thought recognizes in it a metaphysical structure of which one could say in modern terms that it is essentially paradoxical. "For in the final analysis, what is man in nature? A nothing in comparison to the infinite, everything in comparison to nothingness, a mean between nothing and everything. Infinitely far from understanding the extremes, the end of things and their beginning are invincibly hidden from him in an impenetrable secret; he is equally incapable of seeing the nothingness from which he was made and the infinite in which he is swallowed up . . . Let us know, then, our range: we are something and we are not everything; what being we have conceals from us the knowledge of the first principles which are born from nothingness; and the little being we have hides from us the view of the infinite."

Pascal's entire apology will consist in showing that the only real way out of this absolutely desperate situation is the way upwards, that is, in the act by which the creature opens himself to the grace which solicits him.

From Pascal to Kierkegaard, with respect to the problem which occupies us, the passage appears direct, at least to us in the middle of the twentieth century. This does not mean, however, that Pascal exercised a direct influence upon Kierkegaard. The latter certainly knew him, but only quotes him rarely, and it would seem to me rather risky to say that the reading of Pascal contributed in an appreciable way to the formation of Kierkegaard's thought. But what is incontestable is that Pascal appears to *us* as a perfect example of the subjective or existential thinker such as Kierkegaard has defined him in his most important work philosophically, the *Concluding Unscientific Postscript* (*to the Philosophical Fragments*). This existential thinker should be understood in opposition to the abstract thinker whose thought evolves upon the terrain of pure thought and without worrying about the needs or dispositions of his own being. The type of the abstract thinker is, of course, Hegel. On the contrary, the existential thinker is he whose thought is determined by the tasks and the difficulties of his own life, so that it is truly in the service of his existence. He is not disinterested in the sense that the abstract thinker is; rather, he is passionately, he is virtually interested in something which is at the very heart of his existence. And one must add that the subject of this thought is the individual considered in his uniqueness. Kierkegaard can thus write that the task of the subjective or existential thinker consists in understanding himself in existence. This comprehension in existence was already in a certain way the object pursued by Greek thought, but it appears in an entirely new light for the Christian, for whom it is a question of understanding himself in the presence and before the face of God. How can one fail to see that it is to just this comprehension that Pascal wanted to attain. One could, of course, also show that Pascal emerges beyond all philosophy into absolute humility and charity, whereas Kierkegaard remains in spite of everything somehow the prisoner of his own reflection.

Now what is anguish for Kierkegaard?

One could first of all be tempted to think that the phenomenon of anguish is implied for him by the general fact of sin and its consequences. Death is the wages of sin—not only physical death: the eternal death of the soul. It would be natural to admit that anguish is experienced in the presence of this second death, that is, of perdition. It would be a question of anguish of salvation which, after having incited Luther to enter the convent, was later to drive him from it. But the truth is much more complex. An attentive reading of Kierkegaard's treatise on *The Concept of Dread* shows that for the Danish philosopher this phenomenon is situated at the heart of the domain explored by whoever seeks to understand how sin is possible. What results from this profound analysis is that the state of innocence taken in itself already contains the possibility of fault or, if you will, of the fall. "Innocence is ignorance. In it man is not yet determined as mind, but only in his psychism, in unity with what constitutes his nature. The mind is still but in the dream state in him (in other words, he does not have knowledge of the difference between good and evil). This is a situation which still includes peace, quietude. But at the same time there is something here which is not yet either uneasiness or opposition; for there does not yet exist anything which is contested, any dialectic, the mind is not yet dialectic, and it is for this reason that it is not yet real. What is this something?

103

Nothing. But what is the effect of this nothing? It engenders anguish. Such is the profound mystery of innocence: it is at the same time anguish." Anguish is a determination of the dream mind; it is precisely because it is not yet, strictly speaking, a reality that it can dream of this reality which is still but possible. It is the psychology of the child which here comes to our aid and allows us to understand what is in question. We find, indeed, in the child an appetite for adventure, for the unusual, for the mysterious. "This anguish," Kierkegaard says, "belongs so essentially to the child that he does not want to do without it; even if it disturbs him, it enchants him. We find it again in all peoples where childhood has been conserved as a reverie of the mind, and its depth measures the depth of the peoples. Inversely, one can say that the less mind there is, the less anguish."

In the last analysis, what does the mind anguish itself about? This nothing, or more exactly, this near-nothing, is its own abyssal possibility. One is afraid of falling into an abyss, and it is precisely the mind which is this abyss. But we must be sure to understand that it is not at all a question here of a mere abstract thought. This possibility concerns not the definable essence of the mind, but rather its relation to existence. It is as if we were here discovering a dimension of being which could not be recognized by anyone who limited himself to following the path of abstract thought.

It is precisely here that Kierkegaard appears as the true initiator of the philosophy of existence, and it is of the greatest importance to observe at the same time that this philosophy finds itself placed from the outset under the sign of anguish. This is a fact which cannot help but appear disconcerting at first glance. Naturally, one can attempt to explain it by recourse to the peculi-

FROM PASCAL TO KIERKEGAARD

arities of Kierkegaard's life itself. Did he not say in particular
that the strict education given him by his father was destined to
push him headlong into sadness and anguish? We find this
anguish throughout his life, especially in the drama of his engagement which was finally to be broken, and no matter how one
interprets the expression borrowed from St. Paul which he used
so often, "a thorn in the flesh," it is absolutely certain that it is a
question here of a special form of anguish. Nevertheless, this
biographical explanation is obviously insufficient. It can at best
inform us about the particular conditions under which a thought
made its appearance in the individual Kierkegaard—a thought
which was to contribute to the renewal of the philosophical horizon. As Jean Wahl has stated in the note on anguish which he
has appended to his recent book on the philosophies of existence,
"The ideas of anguish and of possibility are intimately connected.
There is in us a knowing which does not entirely know that it is
knowing, for possibility is at once ignorance and knowledge, it is
being and non-being, it is experienced as an anguish." Now, this
presence of good and evil possibilities is the very cause of temptation. "There is," Kierkegaard says, "a captivating anxiety which
fascinates us like the eye of the serpent, and finally pushes us
headlong into the reality of evil."

But whoever says possibility says, in a certain sense, freedom.
Anguish is the vertigo of freedom, but since freedom is caught in
its own snare, and is somehow its own captive, one can and one
must say that we are at once free and determined, at once innocent and guilty. So that Kierkegaard brings out, before Dostoevski, the profound ambiguity which is at the heart of the human
being, considered—we must repeat—not in his essence, as was
the case in classical philosophies, but in his existence, inasmuch

as he exists. One could also express this by saying that the reflection on anguish, that is, on the relation to the nothing, to the near-nothing which is characteristic of the mind, prepares us to understand it not as substance, but as creative process, *as happening,* as activity.

The dialectic which is peculiar to it will be carried on through three distinct spheres of existence. At the aesthetic stage, existence consists in pursuing moments of pleasure permitting one to attain to a certain experienced plenitude. It is Don Juan—and especially the Don Juan of Mozart—who constitutes, as it were, the prototype of this aesthetic existence. And it is indeed the passion of the infinite which already manifests itself here, but in a world which is still but that of the game, of the lie, of infidelity.

He who turns away from this world in order to seek fulfillment in himself attains to ethical existence, and this time it is Socrates who constitutes the model, for he is the man of the saying, "Know thyself." Yet he is still only a witness of the truth, and his doctrine was destined to stiffen into system or purely cynical attitudes.

But at the third stage, the religious stage, man comes to deny himself in the presence of God. This despair is indeed mortal illness, but mortal illness, through the most mysterious paradox, does not lead to death: much to the contrary, it is through despair that the self saves itself, that it attains the eternal and indestructible, precisely because this despair is a mortal leap in the presence of God into the abyss of faith. The weaker man is, the stronger God is in him. The stronger man is, the weaker God is in him. In faith, the transcendent bursts into human reality, which is transfigured into absolute existence.

CHAPTER VIII

From Kierkegaard to Nietzsche and Heidegger

ONE would perhaps not be entirely mistaken in believing oneself able to discover in the thought of Kierkegaard an ambiguity which makes it rather disturbing. Doubtless no one, not even Pascal, has so profoundly analyzed the conditions which must or ought to be met by him who dares to call himself Christian; but to what extent can anyone—including Kierkegaard himself— say that he has met them? In short, between the thought which concentrates on the Christian condition and this condition itself there subsists an interval which can only be crossed by what the Danish philosopher himself, as we have seen, called a leap. But to the eyes of reflection this leap will always appear risky or illegitimate, at the same time as, from the point of view of the Christian, who is on the other side of the gulf, it is obligatory. Whence something like a breach which seems indeed to open in the middle of what one could call the field of human experience. Everything takes place in reality as on an earth shaken by a seismic shock. Since the coming of Christ we live in a split world.

One can thus very well understand that in the light of the most recent history of philosophy and theology, the Kierkegaardian theory of anguish appears, so to speak, bifurcated. It is on the basis of this bifurcation that certain of the recent theological doctrines of the reformed Church have developed, especially those of Karl Barth, those which, in opposition to the liberal Protestantism descended from Kant and Schleiermacher, emphasize above all the absolute transcendence of a God who stands before the believer as the Absolutely Other. These theologies have led, at least in the first phase of Barthism, to a radical humbling of reason before the Word of God, sole bearer of salvation. One can add that even Catholic theologians such as Pryzwara or Guardini have to some extent been influenced by this thought. I will not insist upon all this, which is outside of my subject, and rather will attentively consider the other direction, which the philosophies called existential, and above all that of Heidegger, have taken on the basis of Kierkegaard. Heidegger himself has explicitly acknowledged the importance of the Kierkegaardian conception of anguish. But one must say, I think, that this conception takes root in him in a soil previously tilled by the thought of Nietzsche. It is therefore necessary to ask oneself first of all to what extent the author of *Zarathustra* can himself be considered a philosopher of anguish. The answer to this question is not simple, far from it. I would tend to say that only a psychoanalysis of Nietzschean thought would be able to reveal the role played in it by an anguish not merely repressed, but dominated and as it were heroically subdued. It is self-evident that, even more than for Kierkegaard, the biographical data are here at once very important and insufficient, and in particular that the problem of solitude personally experienced as a trial is at the heart of the Nietzschean tragedy. But in the perspective which I have adopted, what seems to me essential to recall is that the affirmation of the death of God is ascribable in Nietzsche to the tragic consciousness, which is probably not the case, for example, in Sartre. One can, I think, subscribe to what Jaspers writes in the last chapter of his excellent book on Nietzsche:

"The atheism of Nietzsche is the progressive uneasiness of a search for God which perhaps no longer understands itself. The expression given by Nietzsche to his atheism reveals an unspeakable suffering: the necessity of renouncing God is translated by phrases such as this: you will no longer pray, you will no longer rest in an infinite confidence, you forbid yourself to stop before a wisdom, a good, a supreme power and to psalmodize your thoughts . . . Man of refusal, do you want to bear a universal refusal? Who will give you the strength? Does anyone still have this strength? . . ."

"Now," Nietzsche writes on August 2, 1886, to Overbeck, "my life is crossed by the desire that all things be other than I conceive them, that someone make my own truths unworthy of belief to me." "Do you have courage," he asks elsewhere, "not the courage before witnesses, but the courage of the solitary, of the eagle which no god watches any longer?"

Thus the death of God could in no way be envisaged as a fact objectively observed by a historian. In a certain way one could say that it is a question of a certain decision which we have to make, to assume, thus doing violence to a nostalgia for childhood which remains deep down inside a great many of us.

One thus understands the commentary which Heidegger has given in his book, *Die Holzwege*. He there recalls that for Nietzsche we have actually killed God, you and I; that we are all His murderers; and that he asks, "How have we been able to drink the sea? Who gave us the sponge capable of erasing the entire horizon? What have we done by detaching the chain which linked this earth to its sun?" And Heidegger shows that this horizon, this sun, evoke the intelligible world, that of Platonic ideas, if you wish, or of their modern expressions, the world which projected its transfiguring light upon the life of men. But did not Nietzsche declare war once and for all upon these ancestral worlds? Did he not denounce the metaphysical illusion which is expressed in them, and believe that he was thus preparing the way for a transvaluation of values, that is, for the revolution that would find its consummation in the advent of the superman?

I do not think that Heidegger has ever adhered either to the conception of the superman or to that of eternal recurrence. But what he seems to me to retain from Nietzsche is the idea of the consent to finitude, of the abandonment to which we are delivered up in a world into which it seems we have been, so to speak, literally thrown. But as Alphonse de Waehlens very rightly states, Heidegger, seeing that the violence of the negation turns in Nietzsche into affirmation, wanted to be he whose *no* would not bear witness for the *yes,* and esteemed that the establishing of a thought radically delivered from the idea of God could not be conceived by the negation of this idea, but must be formulated without reference to it. I will observe in passing, moreover, that by the avowal of Heidegger himself—and here I refer to what he told me when I talked with him in Fribourg several years ago—it is not fitting to classify him among the atheists, or to regard his doctrine as an atheism. His thought, he said, is in suspense on the problem of the existence of God. It is not certain, of course, that this is his last word. But what is certain is that in his recent works, be it the *Letter on Humanism* or the *Introduction to Metaphysics* which was published in 1953, and in which he again expressed lessons dating from early works, he expressly insists upon the sacred character of Being and in short upon the necessity of restoring this sense of the sacred which the development of philosophy has tended in one way or another to distort or abolish.

But in his analysis or interpretation of the human condition, of man's situation in the world, Heidegger has been led all the same, in the prolongation of Kierkegaard, to see in anguish a category of existence whose importance is fundamental and irreducible.

Let us recall that in his philosophy, I myself exist only insofar as I am in relation with an exteriority which, when it has been organized, will become what I call the world of my experience. In short, I only exist inasmuch as I exist-in-the-world. But this does not mean merely or even essentially that I am in the world as a certain contents in a certain container. The fundamental notion is here that of preoccupation. Every object is defined in relation to a certain type of preoccupation, and it is through such or such particular objects that the exterior world addresses itself to us. Thus for the farmer the world merges with his farm and his field, for the worker with the factory, etc. But it would be an error to see in the world the sum of the objects which it contains; rather, one must explain the objects on the basis of the world. The existent being which I am is defined by the multiplicity of possibilities or of possible actions which are in me; they constitute a network or gridiron which confers a meaning upon things and places them in a certain totality which we call the world. This world is the global sense which my possibilities project upon the background, obscure and devoid of meaning, of raw realities. Let us remark that in this perspective the traditional problem of the reality of the exterior world ceases even

111

to be posed. I would say for myself that Heidegger has shown in a probably definitive way that it is absurd to isolate the existent subject and to ask oneself, on the basis of this subject, whether the world exists or not. For in fact this existent subject is such only in his relation to the world.

But in this context, how does anguish come in? Like Kierkegaard, Heidegger distinguishes it profoundly from fear, which always has a given object: on the contrary, anguish is never provoked by a determined or determinable existent. I quote de Waehlens here again, who, as a matter of fact, limits himself to reproducing the very formulas of Heidegger: "In anguish all the objects of the world and our environment itself suddenly appear devoid, as it were, of all importance, they become ridiculous and collapse into an absolute nullity. I myself feel myself disappearing from the scene inasmuch as I refer to my habitual self made up of preoccupations, ambitions, day-to-day desires . . . What assails us is neither here nor there, since there is no *here* and *there* but in a proximity defined by preoccupation; the menace is everywhere and it is nowhere . . . It is omnipresent. It thus envelops us with a feeling of radical strangeness. Everywhere we are lost and without support. For in the last analysis anguish places us in the presence of the world as world, and not in the presence of such or such an object in the world." But at the same time, anguish is revealed as the calling into question by itself of the being that I am, and we rediscover here, at a perhaps deeper level yet, the identity of anguish and vertigo which Kierkegaard had already recognized.

CHAPTER IX

From Heidegger to Sartr

WE have seen that for Heidegger the finite being that I am loses in anguish its points of support which are situated in the particular things to which particular preoccupations themselves refer. One could say that the anguished person is himself plunged into solitude without recourse in the presence of a world in which he is absolutely not at home. The German term *Unheimlichkeit,* so difficult to translate, here takes on all its significance: it is the world of uprooting and strangeness in which we have no real abode.

What appears clearly is that anguish, far from being a mere affective state, reveals to us our real situation. But this revelation is so tragic that by all possible means we attempt somehow to protect ourselves from it. All the particular modalities which preoccupation affects constitute so many shelters against anguish. But Heidegger also shows with depth how the finite being, dreading to find himself in the presence of his radical finitude, flees into the anonymity of everyday chatter which remains on the surface of existence. Or else into a curiosity, it too completely superficial, which is pursuit of the new for its own sake, distraction, diversion in the Pascalian sense. These are aspects of the inauthentic existence in which each of us degrades himself, usually without even being aware of this degradation.

But from the moment anguish is faced, assumed, it is somehow overcome—and at the same time, the finite being attains to authentic existence. He attains to it in resolution, which does not at all consist in tearing ourselves away from our daily tasks, but delivers us from the tyranny of everyday jobs or preoccupations by permitting us to consider them in a true light. What is this light? One could say that it emanates from our fundamental situation when the latter is clearly acknowledged by a being who has taken anguish upon himself rather than turning away from it. But this situation consists above all in the fact that we are delivered up or doomed to death. The Heideggerian expression *Zum Tode Sein* is very difficult to translate, and I have always wondered whether it did not correspond to a certain ambiguity in the thought, for it does not seem that it should be translated by the word *destination*. It is not a question, strictly speaking, of a finality. Heidegger rather seems to conceive death as the absolute horizon of life. It is this horizon which we have to consider without flinching, and it is in this that resolution consists first of all. But Heidegger goes further still, since for him whoever says finitude says at the same time, in a very profound sense, *culpability,* and it is a question here of a fundamental culpability which has its root in the fact that the finite being— if one can thus express oneself—has as it were a *charge* of nothingness. This culpability too must be courageously, heroically assumed, failing which we sink into the falsehoods of an edulcorated morality or religion.

It would be vain to dissemble the fact that we here find ourselves, as Jean Wahl has very well seen, in the presence of a secularized form of certain traditional theological themes. Everything is as if these themes were loosened or detached from the central affirmations which conferred upon them their justification. What is this fundamental culpability, in fact, if not a transposition of original sin? Just as when Heidegger insists upon the fact that the characteristic of the finite being is to be thrown into the world, it is impossible not to think of the Fall. But the theological presuppositions are voluntarily left aside. One of the principal questions which such a philosophy poses is whether this sort of dissociation is legitimate or not. It must be repeated that Heidegger refuses to be classified among the atheists, that in certain respects his thought presents itself more and more as oriented towards a certain resacralization. And this helps to reinforce the feeling of profound ambiguity which one experiences in reading this difficult philosopher, no doubt the most profound of our time, but the least capable of formulating anything resembling clear directives, of effectively orienting the young people who turn to him as a guide.

When one reads the pages which Jean-Paul Sartre has devoted to anguish in *Being and Nothingness,* though he refers explicitly to Heidegger and even to Kierkegaard, one cannot help but recognize the profound difference of inspiration. This is even clearer in the lecture entitled *L'Existentialisme est un Humanisme.* We here find ourselves in the presence of a man who not only explicitly declares himself an atheist, but who claims—very naïvely, one must admit—to have furnished the proof of the non-existence of God. One could also show without difficulty that this pretension is incompatible with the profound exigency which is at the heart of the philosophies of existence. But I will not insist upon this difficult point. What is important to underline is that if Heidegger presented us with something like the secularization of the thought of Kierkegaard, Sartre provides us with a radically secularized expression of the ideas of Heidegger. But it is probable that he has entirely deformed them in the process, and one cannot wonder that the German philosopher has in recent years repudiated any real affinity with the author of *Being and Nothingness*.

"What does one mean by anguish?" Sartre asks in the lecture which I have alluded to. "The existentialist readily declares that man is anguish. This means: the man who commits himself and who realizes that he is not only he whom he chooses to be, but also a legislator choosing all humanity at the same time as himself, would not be able to escape the feeling of his total and profound responsibility." "Since God does not exist," Sartre also says, "one must deduce the consequences to the bitter end." And the principal consequence is that responsibility is absolute. Since God does not exist, we do not find before us values or orders which legitimize our conduct. Man is condemned at every moment to invent man. Strange thing, Sartre also says here that it is annoying that God does not exist, for along with Him there disappears all possibility of finding values in an intelligible heaven. (We find here again exactly the Nietzschean position which I recalled above.) But in reality one can wonder whether this sort of regret is entirely sincere, and whether on the contrary the existence of God—supposing that it could be established or ascertained—would not be experienced as an unbearable constraint by existentialism *à la* Sartre.

In *Being and Nothingness,* where the analysis is much more elaborate, Sartre undertakes to show that there exists not only an anguish before the future which is related to vertigo, but an anguish before the past, and he here takes as an example the gambler who has freely and sincerely decided not to gamble

116

any more, but who, when he approaches the gaming table, suddenly sees all his resolutions melt away. "What the gambler then grasps in anguish," says Sartre, "is the total inefficacy of the past resolution. It is no doubt there, but frozen, inefficacious, outmoded by the very fact that I am conscious of it. If in a certain way it is I, in a truer sense it is no longer I by the fact that it is for my consciousness. I escape it, it fails in the mission which I had given it, I am it in the mode of not-being." And a little further on, he generalizes in the following way: "This freedom which discovers itself to us in anguish can be characterized by the existence of this trifle which worms itself in between the motives and the act. It is not because I am free that my act escapes the determination of the motives, but on the contrary, the structure of the motives as inefficacious is the condition of my freedom." "In anguish," he will further say, "freedom is anxious before itself inasmuch as it is never entreated or hampered by anything." In general conformity with the thought of Heidegger, Sartre will also show how anguish, which ought to be a permanent state of my affectivity, is in reality exceptional. It is because, in the world of the immediate, we discover ourselves in a world filled with demands, in the midst of projects in the process of realization: I write, I go for a smoke, I have an appointment this evening with Pierre, I must not forget to answer Simon, I have no right to hide the truth any longer from John, etc. And no doubt all these banal and everyday values derive their sense from what Sartre calls a first project of myself, which is in reality the way in which I have chosen myself, or in which I have chosen to be in the world. But all the particular values, all the obligations to which I submit or which I create for myself, come to interpose themselves between

117

me and the consciousness of this original project. They are so many guard-rails to protect against vertigo. "We flee anguish," he says, "by attempting to grasp ourselves from the outside like others or like a thing. One could say that we thus create for ourselves something like permanent alibis, but this is the work of bad faith." "I flee in order to ignore," Sartre further states, "but I cannot ignore that I flee, and the flight from anguish is but a mode of becoming aware of anguish."

One can thus say that Sartre, in a different language, takes up again in a way for his own account the Heideggerian distinction between the inauthentic and the authentic. But the coloration is here completely different, and this appears clearly in a text like this one, which we find at the end of the chapter entitled "Having, Doing, and Being." "He who realizes in anxiety his condition of *being* thrown into a responsibility which veers around until its abandonment, no longer has either remorse, nor regret, nor excuse; he is now only a freedom which discovers itself perfectly and whose being resides in this very discovery." I do not believe I am mistaken in saying that, following the inclination of his temperament, Sartre ends up with an *ethic of unconstraint* which certainly no longer has much in common with that of Nietzsche nor with that of Heidegger. Anguish is here much less assumed than thrown overboard.

CHAPTER X

Goethe and Uneasiness Overcome

I HAVE said that the Sartrean theory of anguish dissolved in the final analysis into a morality of unconstraint. The conclusion of *The Flies* alone seems to me to justify this assertion. You will remember that Orestes, whom the crowd is preparing to stone after the murder of Clytemnestra and Aegisthus, assumes the total responsibility of his crime. He harangues the crowd and evokes the murder of Agamemnon, which its author did not have the courage to assume. "A crime which its author cannot bear is no longer the crime of anyone, is it? It is almost an accident. You welcomed the criminal as your king, and the old crime began to prowl around the city walls, moaning softly like a dog which has lost its master. You look at me, people of Argos, you have understood that my crime is indeed mine; I claim it in the face of the sun, it is my reason for living and my pride, you can neither punish me nor pity me, and this is why I frighten you. And yet, O my men, I love you, and it is for you that I have killed. For you. At present I am one of you, O my subjects, we are bound by blood and I deserve to be your king . . . But have no fear, people of Argos, I will not sit, all bloody, on the throne of my victim: a god offered it to me and I said no. I want to be a king without land and without sub-

jects. Adieu, my men, try to live: everything is new here, everything is to be begun. For me, too, life is beginning."

This text, so fraught with significance, would call for a long
commentary. But what seems obvious is not only that all anguish has here disappeared, but that, in reality, the feeling of
culpability makes room for a sort of boasting which is only possible because Orestes, alias Sartre, has lost all piety, that is, all
sense of divine laws. But under these conditions, the tragic itself
is abolished.

One could show in the same way that the Heideggerian idea
of being-for-death, of being delivered up to death, here undergoes a profound alteration. Sartre here clearly marks, moreover,
his disagreeement with the German philosopher when he declares in *Being and Nothingness* that, "far from death being my
own possibility, it is a contingent fact which, as such, escapes me
by principle, and is from the beginning under the jurisdiction of
my facticity . . . Death is a pure fact, like birth; it comes to us
from without and transforms us within. At bottom, it is in no
way different from birth, and it is the identity of birth and death
which we call facticity." One cannot mark more clearly this will
to desacralization of the conditions of existence which is characteristic of the entire Sartrean enterprise, and which naturally
has as a counterpart a certain exaltation of human freedom. His
thought on this point is certainly ambiguous, since he has written
that we are "condemned to be free," which would lead one to
think that freedom is in no way a conquest, but corresponds
rather to the fact that we are, as I have already said, charged
with nothingness.

It may certainly seem singular, and perhaps even slightly
scandalous intellectually, to now deal without transition with

a man of genius with whom one can be sure that Sartre has never had the least temptation to claim affinity, and for whom I would not even be surprised to learn that he had a special aversion, since Goethe—it is of him that I am thinking—can with difficulty be regarded as a "committed" thinker. The sole transition resides in the fact that in Goethe, if one can speak in a certain way of uneasiness, it does not seem that one could find anything at all which resembles anguish, not even the mastered anguish of which I have spoken regarding Nietzsche.

In his remarkable book on *The Tragedy of Humanism,* Heinrich Weinstock notes the so very significant reaction of Goethe when he learned of the death of Winckelmann, assassinated under atrocious conditions in Trieste in 1768. In the memoir which he dedicates in 1805 to the great aesthetician, he minimizes in the most revealing way the horror of his end in a sordid hotel room, saying that one must esteem him fortunate to have known neither old age nor infirmities, and in short to have been plucked by death at the summit of his existence: a few moments of suffering or fear hardly count, Goethe seems to think, compared with this supreme blessing. Moreover, it is in the same spirit that Goethe signifies his full adhesion to the text in which Lessing, studying the manner in which the ancients imagined death, congratulated them for having seen in it a gentle spirit, a twin brother of sleep.

It is in virtue of the same disposition of mind that Goethe, after the death of Wieland, reproached Falk for having wanted to see the corpse of the poet. "Why," he asks him, "should I let the engaging memories which I have of my friends be spoiled by the cadaveric alteration which their face undergoes? . . . I have been very careful not to see in their coffins either Herder,

121

or Schiller, or the dowager duchess Amalie. Death is one of the most mediocre portrait-painters. For my part, I want to keep in my memory an image of my friends far more animated than that of their death-mask . . . I will not keep it from you, this is precisely what pleases me most in the manner in which Schiller left us. He arrived in Weimar unannounced, and without noise he left. Displays with death are not to my taste."

One can, of course, allege that beneath this preoccupation to avoid all contact with the horrible, the repulsive, lurks a—strictly speaking—repressed anguish, and it is quite possible that this is really so. Nevertheless, what is essentially important in a case like that of Goethe is the way in which the personage has been built up throughout his life and his work. Now it would be, it seems to me, quite difficult, quite risky, to pretend to make any room at all for anguish in this personage. Is the same true for uneasiness? Everything depends on the way in which we define it, and examples such as those of Goethe and also of Gide, of whom I will speak in the next chapter, place us under the obligation of proceeding to more precise discriminations than those which we have used so far.

There is a German word which is rather difficult to translate, but which for Goethe and the German romanticists expressed a profound experience, *Sehnsucht,* which one can translate by aspiration or nostalgia, or nostalgic aspiration. I note, however, that etymologically the word *nostalgia* implies the idea of a desired return, and that the word *Sehnsucht,* in its structure, implies nothing of the sort. But one cannot seriously contest, I believe, that *Sehnsucht* designates a certain form of uneasiness, inasmuch as the French term [*inquiétude*] applies to a certain insatisfaction. I will here quote a very significant poem of Goethe which figures in the *West-östlicher Diwan,* and which is entitled *"Selige Sehnsucht."* Here is the translation, inevitably rather approximate:

> Say to no one but the knowing,
> for the common people immediately mock:
> what I want to praise is that which lives
> and which yearns for fiery death.
> In the cool hours of nights of love
> which begot you, in which you beget,
> you are seized by an unfamiliar sensation
> as the quiet candle glows.
> No more do you remain enveloped
> in the shadow of darkness;
> about you a new longing rages,
> thrusting you to higher generation.
> Distance for you is no deterrent,
> you come flying spellbound,
> and in the end, lustful for light,
> you are burned, oh butterfly.
> And so long as you do not understand this:
> die and come into existence,
> you are but a gloomy guest
> on this darkling earth.

According to Hofmannsthal, this poem was written the very night Christiane Vulpius died, and this would add further to its significant import. It is in exactly the same spirit that Goethe said to Riemer, in the course of conversation, "In everything that lives and is to live, it is necessary that the subject prevail, I mean that it be more powerful than the object. It must get the better of the object, as the flame consumes the wick." This idea of the ascendancy of the subject over the object is obviously the romantic theme par excellence. Among the philosophers, it is Fichte who has developed it the most completely, giving it a principally ethical significance. Among the poets and the mystics, it occurs with very different colorations. But what one must stress above all is that in Goethe this ascendancy of the subject constitutes merely a first period, a first phase which one must transcend. The flame, when it comes to lack objects, can only consume itself; but this sort of self-destruction finds its expression in the very character of Werther. Or rather, as Charles Du Bos has very well stated in his *Aperçus sur Goethe,* "Werther is not a character, not an adventure, not a book, but in all its depth, a fundamental human situation, the negative pole of the very thing of which Goethe's accomplishment represents the positive pole: Werther is the subject, the motive force under pressure which consumes itself for lack of an object." But the unique exploit of Goethe, as Du Bos further states after Berdyaev, is to have made all the subjective side of his being accede to the objective, and it is in this that the second phase consists, that which must follow the initial phase in which the subject, subjectivity, prevails.

Thus is defined the at once so intimate and so particular relation which links Goethe to romanticism. On the one hand, one can certainly not say that Goethe is a romantic, but on the other hand, and perhaps more profoundly, one cannot seriously contest the existence in him of romantic components. There is a Goethean dynamism which finds, of course, its most complete expression in *Faust* and which, in depth, communicates directly with romantic thought, but this dynamism does not exhaust itself in itself, it strives towards the constitution of both the work of art and the personality as work of art, and I believe I am not mistaken in saying that uneasiness, taken in its entirely positive sense, is the internal spring which makes this constitution possible.

CHAPTER XI

Uneasiness in André Gide

I HAVE tried to show that it would be inexact, or in any case rather superficial, to claim that Goethe did not know uneasiness and that it is absent from his work. The truth is infinitely more complex. Under these conditions, one would not be able to subscribe without reserves to André Gide's appraisal of Goethe at the end of his introduction to Goethe's dramatic works in the Pléiade edition. "Before his death-mask, in which his eyelids have closed forever upon so much inner serenity, I evoke the ravaged or tragic and sorrowful masks of Dante, of Pascal, of Beethoven, of Nietzsche, of Leopardi: their voice is the more throbbing. . . . After Goethe had his fill of everything which is possible on earth, by speaking of renunciation does he want to give us to understand that his arms were still wider than his embrace? That he could have embraced more? Or would not the far graver question be this: Did Goethe embrace the best? And what is the best for man, to which nothing must be preferred? It belongs to Christians alone to ask this primary and supreme question. That it could not alter the serenity of Goethe, this is precisely what is important for us. And Goethe would no longer be Goethe if uneasiness or suffering had added the pathos of a few wrinkles to the patiently acquired calm of this admirable effigy."

But the very fact that this calm was "patiently acquired" indicates sufficiently that, if uneasiness has been overcome, it is much rather to the extent that it has been incorporated into the life and the work of art. In this perspective it is singularly instructive to compare a text like the sublime *Marienbader Elegie* to the last works of Gide, in which no uneasiness quivers any longer, and which offer us the disconcerting—I would even say, for my part, anguishing—spectacle of a man to whom it seems to have been given, one must say, to deliver himself not only from all expectation, but from all fervor. The Gide of the 1940's makes us think of Voltaire—but of a Voltaire perhaps even more cynical than the author of *Candide*—much rather than of the author of *Faust*.

And yet, when we go back to his first works, what place does uneasiness not seem to occupy in them, uneasiness in almost all its forms and with all its timbres. I am not thinking here above all of the *Cahiers d'André Walter,* and of the mixture of agitation and religiosity which distinguishes this youthful work, which Gide himself was to judge so severely in 1930. He does not repudiate it and is willing to believe what certain people tell him: that he is already present in it almost in his entirety. But it is of its defects that he is mainly sensible, of its lacks which often disclose him, but also sometimes betray him. "What I suffer from the most in rereading my *Cahiers* is a complacency with myself which leaves every sentence insipid." Certain passages of the *Journal* which are contemporary with the *Cahiers* are perhaps more profoundly significant. This one, for example, which dates from January 3, 1892:

"Will I always torment myself like this, and my mind, Lord, will it from now on rest in no certitude? Like a sick person in his bed, who tosses and turns in order to find sleep, I worry from morning to night. And even at night uneasiness wakens me. I worry about not knowing who I will be. I do not even know who I want to be. But I know well that one must choose. I would like to walk along sure paths, or even merely where I would have liked to go. But I do not know; I do not know what I should want. I sense a thousand possibilities in myself, but I cannot resign myself to only wanting to be one of them. And I am frightened, every instant, at every word that I write, at every gesture that I make, to think that it is one more trait, ineffacable, of my face which is fixed; a hesitant, impersonal, a weak face, since I have not known how to choose and delimit it proudly."

One sees clearly here that uneasiness is linked at once to the sense of the possible, to the necessity of a choice which runs the risk of mutilating him who makes it, and also no doubt to the fear lest this inevitable sacrifice somehow take place of itself under impure conditions which do not correspond to the most profound exigency of being—that exigency which has so much trouble apprehending itself.

A note of October 10, 1893, shows Gide ceasing to call his desires temptations, ceasing to resist them, and doing his best, on the contrary, to follow them. "Self-renunciation seemed to me a superior wisdom: it seemed to me that I would find in it the greatest benefit for my being. This was still, I know, an egoism, but newer, more curious, and which satisfied more forces in me. I retain this word: satisfy forces, that was at present my morality. And then I no longer wanted any morality, I wanted to live powerfully."

Here appears what will be Gide's immoralism, an immoralism which will attempt in many cases to present itself as a superior morality, a morality which at certain moments will even claim quite paradoxically to rejoin authentic Christianity, a Christianity not covered up and altered by dogmas and theology.

"The necessity of option was always intolerable to me," we read at the beginning of the fourth book of *Les nourritures terrestres*. "To choose seemed to me not so much choosing as rejecting what I did not choose." "To choose was to renounce forever, for always, all the rest—and the large quantity of this rest remained preferable to no matter what unit. Thence came, moreover, a little of my aversion for no matter what *possession* on earth: the fear of at once no longer possessing but that."

We are here, I think, at the very heart of what was Gide's uneasiness: it is not above all insatisfaction, but the refusal of satisfaction. For satisfaction always implies a certain contentment with what one has and by this very fact, somehow, a subservience to having. It is furthermore in this, it seems to me, no doubt through a delusion which is not very difficult for us to uncover, that Gide was for a long while able to believe that he had remained a disciple—heterodox, to be sure, but a disciple all the same—of Christ. He was not able to see, or did not want to understand, that the ethic of the instant which was long his was linked much rather to the voluptuous hedonism of an Omar Khayyam than to the morality of the Gospel.

Nonetheless, in the presence of a personality as complex as this one, we certainly have to forbid ourselves all simplifications, all schematizations, which would imply the non-recognition of this very complexity. It would not only be absurd, it would be iniquitous to want to underestimate the role which Dostoevski, at a certain period, played in the thought of Gide. And on the other hand, it is too evident that the exaltation of the instant of *Les nourritures terrestres* is totally foreign to the universe of Dostoevski. I will even add that it is incompatible with what

Unamuno has called the tragic sense of life—and one can hardly maintain that this sense was purely and simply foreign to the author of *Straight Is the Gate*. The very text that I quoted at the beginning of this study sufficed to show that Gide, at least during the greatest part of his life, felt a genuine respect—and perhaps it is even a question here of a more ardent, more glowing feeling than respect—for certain of the greatest representatives of the tragic consciousness: a Pascal or a Dostoevski, for example. In this perspective, one must say, I think, that the uneasiness in Gide, at least at certain moments—but moments which it is perfectly possible for us to spot—, took on the character of an authentic anguish. The essential text here is the intimate work which he entitled *Num quid et tu?*, which one must complete by an essential page of the *Feuillets* and also by the book which Gide devoted to Dostoevski.

If we manage to forget the last period of Gide's life, which I would be inclined—alas!—to call the sort of inner mummification to which his final journals bear witness, we cannot read without emotion this page dated June 16, 1916: "I no longer know how to pray, or even to listen to God. If He perchance speaks to me, I do not hear. I have become completely indifferent to His voice. And yet I have the disdain of *my* wisdom, and for want of the joy which He gives me, all other joy is taken from me.

"Lord, if You are to help me, what are You waiting for? I cannot alone. I cannot.

"All the reflections of You which I felt in me are growing dim. It is time that You come.

"Ah! Do not let the Evil One in my heart take Your place! Do not let Yourself be dispossessed, Lord! If You withdraw, he installs himself. Ah, do not confuse me entirely with him! I do not love him as much as that, I assure You. Remember that I was able to love You."

A note of September 19, 1916, is still more moving:

"I am the drowning person who loses courage and no longer defends himself except feebly. The three summons have the same sound: It is time. It is high time. It is too late. So that one does not distinguish them one from the other, and the third is already sounding while one believes himself still at the first.

"If I could at least tell this drama, paint Satan after he has taken possession of a being, using him, acting through him upon others . . ."

And then this: "I took for good everything which was well-regulated. By moderation I thought I would overcome evil; and it is by means of this moderation, on the contrary, that the Evil One was taking possession of me."

"Unfortunate," he will further write October 3, "who pretend to unite in yourself heaven and hell. One only gives oneself to God in one's entirety."

Even if Gide later repudiated these thoughts, and this is not a matter of doubt, it is essential to know that he was able to form them: for it is not a question simply of an idea, but of an intimate and tragic experience, an experience which, under conditions which remain to be elucidated, he was later to make a point of obliterating. But there are perhaps few examples in the life of great minds of cases in which the option, the free choice, appear as visibly. It is to my eyes perfectly clear that Gide, no doubt to a great extent under the pressure of what was not at the outset, but later became a sexual fatality, freely chose against God. And in this sense, the Gide of the final period, that of *Œdipe* and of *Thésée,* comes in a way to join the Sartre of *The Flies.*

130

CHAPTER XII

Uneasiness in the World of Today

I HAVE finished the inventory, as incomplete as it is, of the forms which uneasiness and anxiety have taken on in the great minds whose thought cannot leave us indifferent, even if it does not obtain our adhesion.

But it must be recognized that we have to adopt a position ourselves today. I add that the present situation summons us to pose the problems in terms which are no longer entirely those in which our predecessors formulated them. I would like to indicate here wherein it seems to me that this transformation consists.

Whether or not one is right to interpret in an optimistic sense the fact that the most concrete great problems are today posed on a world-wide scale, it is beyond doubt that this broadening of scope presents for the question which occupies us a primordial importance. Much more than the men of the nineteenth century, we see ourselves today under the obligation of interrogating ourselves upon the future of humanity, or more exactly, upon the significance which it is or is not possible to attach to the human adventure considered as a whole. The repercussion of what takes place at certain nerve-centers of the earth's crust upon the destiny of the entire species can no longer be contested but by those who seek to blindfold themselves voluntarily. To be sure, for at least two thousand years there has been no lack of thoughtful minds to adopt as their own the phrase of Terence: "I esteem that nothing human could be foreign to me." But this assertion offered but a moral and, in short, ideal significance. Nowadays it must be taken literally, and it bears upon our entire destiny, I mean upon the destiny of each of us. Each of us is called upon to become aware that his personal life can be disrupted from top to bottom following events which take place in a part of the world where he has never set foot and of which he perhaps only forms the vaguest of images. In this respect, the Korean affair constitutes a date which, despite appearances, is no doubt no less critical than the Spanish Civil War, the latter having no doubt marked a major stage in contemporary history, since it is beginning with it that the distinction between civil war and international war has tended to be obliterated.

What are the consequences of this state of affairs as far as uneasiness is concerned? It seems that each of us must give up constituting within himself a little world under cover, a little enclosed world, behind partitions whose imperviousness is assured by a set of precautions of all kinds. I do not mean, of course, that the illusion of living in a world of this kind has completely disappeared, either in France or in neighboring countries. But even where it persists, it is shaken, it is undermined. No one can henceforth be completely protected against a certain disorder, a certain malaise, which corresponds to this disturbance. All that one can say is that where this trouble is felt, it is ordinarily badly interpreted, perhaps not even interpreted at all. One would not be completely mistaken, although this affirmation must be delicately shaded, in saying that in a certain perspective the Communist thrust translates, in a unilateral way, the leverage exercised upon the world of existences closed and shut in upon themselves by another world still to be born, but which seems indeed to have to constitute itself in antagonism to that of private life. It is not a question, however, of abandoning oneself either to prophecies or even to an appraisal of what this world will be worth if it manages to materialize entirely. Let us observe, moreover, that it has already taken shape to a certain extent, but under conditions which give rise to almost infinite contestations: in the present state of affairs, it partakes at once of the order of fact, of that of project, and even of that of myth. This hybrid existence has a great deal to do with the pressure that it exerts everywhere.

One must immediately add, however, that what I have just said does not apply exclusively to the Soviet world or to the world in the process of Sovietization—but also, although in a slightly different way, to the American world or the world in the process of Americanization. Here too, although on a far more strictly economic and less ideological plane, we are faced with a world which presents itself fundamentally as an enterprise, some will even say an imperialism, and this word cannot be entirely brushed aside, although it calls for several reserves. Let us rather say that it cannot be used in both cases with the same rigor, since in one case it bears above all upon the obtaining of a world-wide clientele, whereas in the other it applies to the establishment on a world-wide scale of one and the same way of living and thinking.

But what seems to me essential for our subject is that despite these differences there exists between Sovietism and Americanism a close convergence, for in both we discover the pretension, as exorbitant as it may be, of establishing everywhere a state of affairs which tends to get rid of uneasiness and anguish. If one is willing to reflect upon it, one will perceive that there exists in both cases one and the same orthodoxy which cannot put up with uneasiness, and which even goes so far as to treat it as amenable to certain treatments—the nature of which varies, however, from one camp to the other.

On the American side, psychoanalysis is not only admitted but encouraged and even propagated as much as possible. On the Soviet side, on the contrary, it is excluded at least temporarily, and for doctrinal reasons. One can doubt, however, that the ostracism which weighs upon it is definitive, and I would be tempted to wonder whether it does not correspond to an error of interpretation, but I will not insist upon this point.

For what one can call the official American psychoanalysis, uneasiness is at once a disorder—and the sign of a still deeper disorder which seems indeed to be situated at the frontier of the individual and the social. One makes it a matter of principle that uneasiness translates a genuine functional defect, the origin of which the psychoanalyst is *a priori* certain to be able to locate. At the limit, there is no great difference between him and the mechanic who is called upon to give his opinion upon the causes of a given irregularity in the functioning of a motor, for example. One puts oneself into the hands of the psychoanalyst, as one entrusts one's automobile to the mechanic. It is obvious that a philosophy of behavior (behaviorism), for which what we call the inner life is but an illusion or a kind of inconsistent nebulousness, is necessarily led to minimize this difference.

But how can one help but see, on the other hand, that in a world in which Marxist materialism has triumphed, it is in the final analysis also a philosophy of behavior and adaptation which must inevitably prevail. All that one can say is that the treatment

134

to which one will in this case subject the uneasy or anxious person will present a more directly punitive character. But I would personally be inclined to believe that, in the final analysis, this is merely a nuance perhaps destined to fade away in coming years, if a war or a revolution does not come to hamper the consolidation of one regime or the other.

We are apparently quite far from the considerations to which we have seen a Kierkegaard or a Nietzsche, or even a Heidegger, abandon himself. As far as Sartre is concerned, it does not appear at all certain to me that what I have called an ethics of unconstraint is not destined to emerge, by the most singular paradox, into a philosophy of conditioning. By putting freedom everywhere Sartre, unawares, perhaps comes in the final analysis to suppress it.

But it appears clearly that the principal question, a question easier to formulate than to solve, is that of knowing whether one should attribute a positive value to uneasiness or not. I say to uneasiness, not to anguish. We have seen several times that in the last analysis one can neither identify them nor establish a precise line of demarcation between them. But what we have also been able to ascertain is that if one can speak of a fruitfulness of uneasiness, it seems far more difficult to express oneself in this way regarding anguish. I will come back to this point at the end of our study.

But let us ask ourselves at present in the name of what postulate one can be led to treat uneasiness, whatever it be, as a pathological datum.

Let us carefully observe that this condemnation will no longer be made today as among the ancients, in the name of an aristocratic ethics of impassibility, but in a bio-sociological perspective which is that of efficiency. One will begin with the fact, considered indisputable, that a person prey to uneasiness does not find himself under the conditions which permit any worker to furnish a satisfactory output. In order to carry out a task well, whatever it be, one must be able to abandon oneself to it with all one's heart. But this is just what uneasiness does not permit. From a psycho-pathological point of view, one will say that it is perhaps something rather analogous to a nascent schizophrenia. This occasions, in particular, very precise consequences as far as the attitude towards death is concerned. To preoccupy oneself with death, to meditate on it and its significance, will be regarded as the act of a morbid consciousness. I was told years ago that an American lady on her way to Europe with her daughter having died during the crossing, the chance friends of the young lady did not rest till she had danced with them, so as to dispel the sad thoughts, the morbid thoughts, that this death was in danger of developing in her. The "funeral parlors" where one is accustomed to display the corpse of the dead, nicely dressed, "resting" in an atmosphere of luxury and piped music, correspond to an entirely analogous preoccupation. It is a question of not making the living gloomy, and for that, either of repressing or of camouflaging certain sinister realities, the awareness of which would be in danger of making them less fit for life. We have here, strange to tell, a sort of burlesque and grimacing translation of the famous theorem of Spinoza, that "there is nothing which men should think less about than death."

In a Marxist moral climate, a fundamentally comparable attitude will present itself under a rather different aspect. The mixture of jazz and nauseating sentimentality which legitimately horrifies us in certain American customs is certainly missing. What tends to establish itself is a mentality according to which a person who has accomplished his task, who has fulfilled his function, must give place without anguish, nay without sadness, to those who are destined to succeed him, to provide in their turn a contribution to the edification of the new society. Uneasiness will be regarded here above all as a sort of residue of infantile, bourgeois, and in short unhealthy beliefs which the people no longer needs once it is emancipated.

I will add that from the moment man is considered as a simple functional unit, this conception appears perfectly logical and even irrefutable. The whole thing is to know whether it can really be accepted.

Conclusion

In order to know what one must finally think of uneasiness, it is thus fitting to ask oneself whether the human being can be regarded as a mere functional unit. No one will be able to dispute, indeed, that if one adopts this perspective, uneasiness—even the highest uneasiness—must be regarded as a defect or as linked to a defect. I have just said *even the highest uneasiness;* but one must immediately add that such a way of expressing onself implies a hierarchy of values, the principle of which can only be discovered outside of all reference to a functioning of any kind.

I attempted to show a long while ago, in a text that was re-published a few years ago, that in a world in which the functional triumphs on all planes, the meaning of being is almost inevitably obliterated. I will quote several lines from this text: "It is an impression of oppressive sadness which emanates from a world centered upon function. It suffices to evoke the heart-breaking image of the pensioner as well as the obviously connected image of city Sundays when the strollers give the impression of being pensioned off from life . . . But there is not only the sadness of this spectacle for the one who looks at it, there is the dull, the intolerable malaise felt by the one who sees himself reduced to living as if he were indeed identical with his functions. And this malaise suffices to prove that there is an atrocious error or abuse of interpretation which a more and more inhuman social order, and a philosophy inhuman as well, have equally tended to instill in defenseless intelligences . . . Life in a world centered upon the idea of function is exposed to despair, because in reality this world is empty, because it rings hollow; if it resists despair, it is solely to the extent that certain secret powers, which it is unable to conceive or to recognize, are at work at the heart of this existence and in its favor . . ."

The person who finds himself engaged in this world of functions, whether it be a question of organic, psychological, professional, or social functions in the broadest sense, experiences deep within himself the need that there be *being,* that is to say, that everything not be reduced to a game of successive and inconsistent appearances, or, to repeat the famous phrase of Shakespeare, to "a tale told by an idiot."

But I think that I can make it a matter of principle that uneasiness and the aspiration to being are today closely interdependent. It is possible that it has not always been so. I am thinking of civilizations of the sacral type, like thirteenth-century France, in which the fundamental values commanding the very structure of institutions were still religious values. This can raise objections of an historical order, and it would perhaps be wiser to stick to a hypothetical formulation: admitting that a civilization of the sacral type is possible, it seems that it does not imply the connection between uneasiness and the meaning of being which appears, on the contrary, where, as in our own world, the essential values present themselves as the object of contestation. I will observe, moreover, that the totalitarian states present us with a dreadful counterfeit of the civilizations of the sacral type. Uneasiness, as we have seen, is here prohibited and sometimes persecuted; but in a sacral civilization it would not arise, any more than clouds would be able to form in a country where a dry and sunny climate prevails.

In this perspective, one can discern rather well what judgment it is fitting to make upon uneasiness. Let us not go so far as to say that it is good in itself, and above all let us not say so of anguish. This could be a dilettantism which I, for my part, reject. But what is exact is first of all that the absence of uneasiness, except perhaps in the saint, is a serious symptom. If I except the case of the saint, it is because where faith is absolute it seems that there is immunization against uneasiness. Yet this is true only at the extreme: first of all because there is certainly no faith which does not know certain eclipses, but also and above all because the saint does not appear to himself as a saint; sanctity can only be recognized by the Church or by a posterity which acts as Church. But the humility which is one of the attributes of the saint cannot go without a certain uneasiness about oneself. We can make a generalization: a soul to which all uneasiness about oneself is foreign is a soul affected with sclerosis.

One can hardly contest the fact that the reasons for each one of us to be uneasy about himself have gained considerably in strength in the contemporary period. In the light of psychoanalysis or of what is called depth psychology, we have to acknowledge that we are not clear about our inmost being and our possibilities.

The same is true, furthermore, as far as the others are concerned, at least to the extent that we consider them as objects of knowledge. Let us remark, however, that where it is a question of those close to us, of those with whom we maintain intimate relations, and where from this fact a repsonsibility devolves upon us, it is doubtful that we have, I do not say the power, but the right to adopt the strictly objective attitude of one who merely seeks to know. This does not mean that we are bound not to know the true nature of those close to us, or to take pleasure in an illusion of any kind. This simply signifies, as Christianity has marvelously understood it, that the relations here go beyond the plane of pure intelligence, and if it were otherwise the very notion of responsibility would be void of sense. Let us not conclude from this that uneasiness can here be eliminated, but rather that it should be transmuted into an active disposition which partakes of faith. I am thinking, for example, of the uneasiness which each of us can feel before the physical and moral development of his children. But I would add that faith can by no means be conceived in a quietist sense, it must on the contrary stir up as it were a continual invention, which could not be the case where uneasiness becomes anguish, for anguish, despite what has been said about it—and I again insist upon it in conclusion—can but paralyze him who feels it, above all when he takes pleasure in it.

These considerations apply to a great extent to uneasiness in as far as it has to do with exterior events. When we evoke the catastrophic possibilities which seem to block our horizon, anguish can appear inevitable, and I add that it almost merges with fear. It is indeed fear which takes hold of us at the thought of the monstrous weapons which can tomorrow destroy everything which constitutes our reasons for living. If this fear is interiorized in uneasiness, it is, it seems to me, to the extent to which each of us has the obscure feeling that he ought to be able to prevent a cataclysm which draws its origin from man

himself, and that we all have as it were an imponderable responsibility in the event which we dread. This feeling should
not, however, be artificially overestimated. I merely think that
each of us ought to be careful in the strictest way not to say or
do anything which would contribute the slightest bit to the
chances of war. Unfortunately, experience teaches us that there
exists a certain pacifism based on illusion which in fact plays
in favor of violence, and this we have already seen in the era of
Hitlerism. It is perhaps simply by always making a point of
seeing the present reality in a light of truth, that is, as objectively as possible, that we can strugggle the most effectively for
peace. It is a fact that fostered equivocation or ambiguity always serves the designs of the powers of war; and the inverse
is true of a certain intrepid lucidity.

I will not fail, on the other hand, to recall that there is another
plane, that of faith, of hope, of charity, that of prayer, which
is perhaps the only one on which one can serve peace by establishing it first of all in oneself. But all that we have previously
seen also shows us that on this plane, uneasiness cannot be
eluded, but only overcome. I will be still more explicit, at the
risk of shocking certain of my readers. At the same time as
we struggle for peace by human means, we have, I think, always to assure ourselves more intimately of the reality of the
invisible world. And this brings me back to what I have already
pointed out. Positive uneasiness, that which presents a value
in itself, is the disposition which allows us to detach ourselves
from the vise in which daily life squeezes us, with its hundreds
of cares which end up by masking the true realities. *This* uneasiness is a principle of self-transcendence, it is a path which
we have to ascend in order to attain to true peace, to that which

no dictatorship, no imperialism, has the power of disturbing, for in the most precise sense peace is not of this world, and it is likely that of *this* peace the powerful could not have the least notion. I have said uneasiness, not anguish, for when all is said and done I rather believe that I will deny, personally, the Kierkegaardian affirmations: it seems to me that anguish is always an evil, since it is after all closed in upon itself, and at the same time it is in danger, as we have seen, of giving birth to a sort of sadistic delight, whether or not one should see in it, with certain psychoanalysts, something like the manifestation of the need of self-puishment.

In my opinion, and I do not say it without hesitation, the philosophies of existence founded on anguish have seen their day, and it is strongly to be feared that they lead to a dead-end. If they can renew themselves, it is, I am convinced, by means of a meditation on hope and on joy. I have said *joy,* not satisfaction, for the latter only concerns having, and is no doubt linked to what is most perishable in us. But joy, whatever one might think of it, does not exclude uneasiness such as we have seen it in particular define itself for a St. Augustine. For this uneasiness is after all the aspiration of a minus-being towards a plus-being, and it is quite possible that it can only find its term beyond the narrow limits within which our apparent existence goes on, in a loving contemplation which can only be a participation. If man is essentially a voyager, it is because he is *en route,* as one of my characters says in *L'Emissaire,* "towards an end which one can say at once and contradictorily that he sees and does not see." But it is indeed uneasiness which is the inner spring of this progression, and no matter what those say about it who, in the name of a technocratic ideal, claim to prohibit it, man cannot lose this stimulus without becoming immobilized and dying. One will no doubt readily agree, it is true, that even technical progress supposes a certain stimulation of this kind, and it is indisputable. But what we have to recall in the name of a higher exigency, is that this technical progress, whatever it may be, cannot suffice unto itself, and that it degenerates into a ridiculous game if it does not remain dependent on the affirmation of a reign of charity which assures—under conditions but imperfectly representable—that unity of all in all of which what Christian theology calls the "mystical body" presents us with the only notion susceptible of satisfying us, I will even say of quenching our thirst.